CW00829649

Voices From Cave Hill

Ben Simon

Best wishes,

Ben Simon.

I would like to thank all of the people who kindly contributed stories for this publication. They have brought to life memories that would otherwise have been lost. Each person was tape recorded separately, generally in their home over cups of tea, during the period 2006 to 2010. The recordings were transcribed and edited as lightly as possible, retaining many of the grammatical errors we all make when speaking to try to retain the character of the storyteller. At a followup meeting the text was discussed with the contributor to allow for any changes or additional information. Many of the recollections of one person are collaborated by another, though memory is always fickle and there are a few discrepancies which have not been removed. A short introduction has been given at the beginning of each section to provide a setting for the stories and further information is included in the Notes and References section at the end of the book. If you have any other stories, documents or pictures that might help us discover more about the heritage of Cave Hill please contact the Cave Hill Conservation Campaign via the website: www.cavehillconservation.org or e-mail John Gray, who is currently working on a full-length history of Cave Hill, at: j.gray310@ntlworld.com

This project was undertaken as part of the Living Landscapes scheme of the Forest of Belfast. I am grateful for the encouragement given by the Forest of Belfast Steering Group and the support given by Robert Scott of Belfast City Council, John Gray and Cormac Hamill of the Cave Hill Conservation Campaign, Jim Bradley of the Belfast Hills Partnership and Sue Christie of Northern Ireland Environment Link. John Fisher of Belfast Zoo and the staff at Belfast Castle including Fintan Grant and the team of grounds staff also kindly assisted in many ways.

I would like to thank Maura Pringle, cartographer at Queen's University School of Geography, Archaeology and Palaeoecology and staff at the Public Record Office of Northern Ireland (PRONI), Linenhall Library, Queen's University Library and Belfast Central Library for their assistance in my research for this publication. Robert Scott and John Gray kindly commented on drafts of the text and I am very grateful to Elita Frid for proofreading.

Alex and our daughter Lucia, thank you both for your patience and support.

Ben Simon, 9 October 2010

Voices From Cave Hill

Ben Simon

2010

THE FOREST OF
BELFAST

ISBN 978-0-9551583-3-9

A publication of the Forest of Belfast, 89 Loopland Drive, Belfast BT6 9DW.

Design by Cheah Design.
Printed and bound in the UK by the MPG Books Group, Bodmin and King's Lynn.

Published with the support of

Discovering Cave Hill

Cave Hill forms an instantly recognisable backdrop to Belfast and is famous for its profile: the outline of a face gazing skywards, often described as Napoleon's Nose. This tradition can be traced back at least to the early decades of the 19th century and its origins may be much older; some assert that the profile of the hill provided the inspiration for Jonathan Swift to write Gulliver's Travels.[1] The hill is also famous for several small caves on the cliffs, though there remains a debate whether they are largely natural or man-made and, if cut by human hand, what purpose did they serve?[2]

There are intriguing old stories of treasure on Cave Hill: of valuables stored in the caves and of fairy gold hidden in chests upon the summit of Cave Hill that only the seventh son of a seventh son might be able to find.[3, 4] Yet another tale concerns the Cave Hill Diamond, a massive gem (said by some to have belonged to no less than Finn McCool) hidden somewhere on the hill.[5] These stories tell us that Cave Hill has long been considered a place of secrets that awaited discovery.

Hills have a special place in the traditions of Ireland and on the summit of Cave Hill there used to be a feature referred to in one description as '...some large stones... piled together so as to form a seat', and by others as a stone throne.[6] Cave Hill was also the place where crowds gathered every Easter for festivities that included dancing, eating and drinking, and rolling coloured eggs – revelry that George Benn, author of *The History of the Town of Belfast* (1823), considered had been taking place at this site from time immemorial.[7]

Cave Hill is bound up with the history of Belfast. It was at McArt's Fort, the earthworks on the summit of Cave Hill, that Wolfe Tone and his companions met to assert the independence of Ireland prior to the 1798 Rebellion.[8] It was also to Cave Hill that the Belfast Troop of Light Dragoons, Belfast Volunteer Company and Belfast Artillery Company marched in 1782, fired a royal salute, pitched tents and after dinner 'toasts were drank in native whiskey, diluted with water issuing from one of the finest springs in the universe'.[9] This, in all probability, was the spring by one of the paths up the hill that is still known as the Volunteers' Well.

The attachment that Belfast people have for Cave Hill was put to the test when, in 1855, the traditional route up the hill above Gray's Lane was blocked by a landowner. This prompted the formation of The Association for the Protection of Public Rights of Way which in 1859 won a legal battle to assert the right of access.[10] With public access guaranteed, Cave Hill became a focus for tourists wishing to gain a panoramic view of the city and for outings by groups including geologists, the Belfast Arts Society and Belfast Field Naturalists' Society.[11]

Today Cave Hill is a country park and the entirety of the uplands is open to all. It attracts locals and visitors throughout the year and something of the old Easter traditions still remains: the first warm weekends of early spring witness an outpouring of Belfast residents eager to escape the city and stretch their legs on Cave Hill. Also at Easter many families still take their children to the hill clutching bags or hoop-handled wicker baskets of hard-boiled eggs. The eggs – some intricately decorated, some plain or with felt pen faces – are trundled down slopes, quickly followed by squealing children who gather them up to repeat the task until the grass is covered in broken shells and bits of egg.[12] Recently, a new story has provided added significance for visitors to the hill. This surrounds the discovery of a gold wedding ring at the site of a wartime crash of an American B17 Flying Fortress. This find, on the wooded slopes near the zoo, symbolises in a unique way the tragedy of war.

This publication comprises memories of Cave Hill, told by people who know the area well. They bring the past to life, describing the area, the buildings and people who lived on the land. Some of these stories have shed new light on the history of the hill. For example, when this project started, none of the Belfast Parks staff knew that within living memory there had been a gamekeeper in the Castle Estate, living with his family in a house deep in the woods. The story of a little wooden house independently referred to by two contributors as the Shaftesbury children's playhouse was also a complete surprise and provides us with a tiny glimpse into the private lives of the Shaftesbury family. The memories of Jean Martin, a Wren at Belfast Castle when it was requisitioned by the Admiralty, provide fascinating and previously unrecorded details of Belfast's war history. These stories will hopefully encourage others to delve deeper, to explore the area on foot and through the archives, and discover more about our heritage.

The stories told of Cave Hill have been grouped into accounts of four contrasting areas. The first is Carr's Glen, an attractive valley on the southern end of Cave Hill that is now well-wooded but which within living memory was largely farmed fields. The next section comprises recollections of the tiny communities of cottages known as Daddystown and Mammystown that lay on the Cave Hill well above Belfast, between the top of Carr's Glen and the old quarry workings to the north. The third group of stories are about the central part of Cave Hill Country Park, the lands of the former estate of the Donegall and Shaftesbury families that surround Belfast Castle. Finally, some memories are recorded about Bellevue including the amusements, pleasure gardens, zoo and Floral Hall, places of entertainment created near the top of the Antrim Road and advertised as 'Belfast's Mountain Playground'.

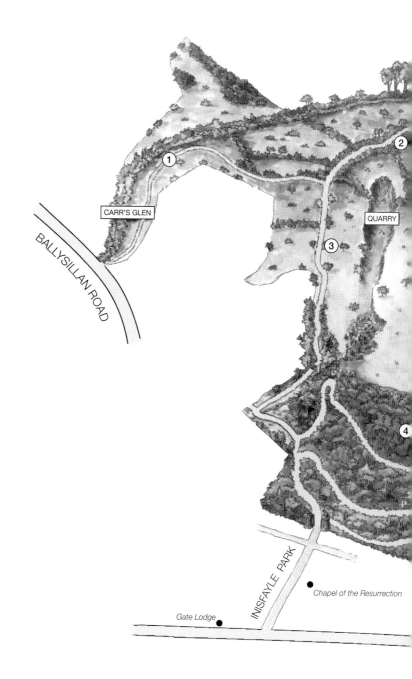

Site of some former buildings and half-forgotten places

1 Carr's Glen Mill
2 Daddystown
3 Mammystown
4 Gamekeeper's cottage
5 Martlett Towers
6 Castle stables and Hill House
7 Floral Hall
8 Grand staircase

Some buildings near the Antrim Road that were constructed for the Belfast Castle Estate and are now privately owned are also shown.

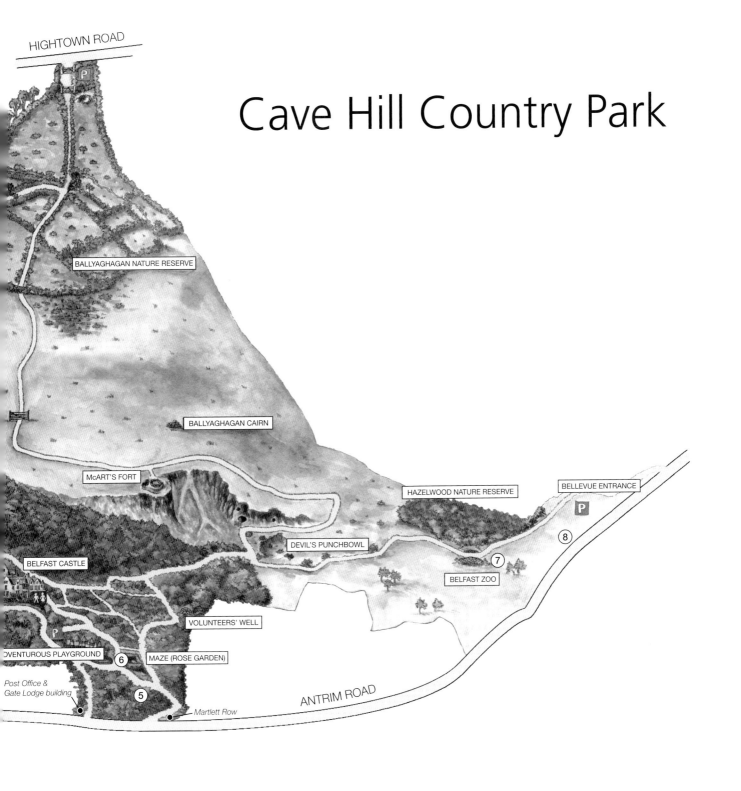

Cave Hill Country Park

HIGHTOWN ROAD

BALLYAGHAGAN NATURE RESERVE

BALLYAGHAGAN CAIRN

McART'S FORT

HAZELWOOD NATURE RESERVE

BELLEVUE ENTRANCE

DEVIL'S PUNCHBOWL

BELFAST CASTLE

BELFAST ZOO

VOLUNTEERS' WELL

ADVENTUROUS PLAYGROUND

MAZE (ROSE GARDEN)

Post Office &
Gate Lodge building

Martlett Row

ANTRIM ROAD

Carr's Glen

Carr's Glen, Belfast.   A picturesque bit in the upper part of the glen.

Carr's Glen is said to have taken its name from the family of Henry Carr, a merchant, who in 1692 leased land at Ballysillan, then known as Glinmullen from Lord Longford, Arthur, Earl of Donegall and others. The land passed to a nephew of Henry, James Carr, and later to David Lyons of Old Park who married the daughter of James Carr. The river that flows through the glen was used by local industries and also supplied the Water Commissioners' Antrim Road Waterworks, a situation that gave rise to a number of lawsuits.[13]

The 1857 six-inch Ordnance Survey map of the area shows that at this time there were two mills upstream of the Ballysillan Road, both with sizeable mill ponds, both described as flour mills. In a revision of 1901 only one mill is shown, and this had the title of 'Glencarr Beetling Mills'. Beetling mills were used to finish linen cloth by pounding it with lengths of timber known as beetles that were set vertically in a frame and, using water power, repeatedly lifted and dropped onto the cloth. A well-known early postcard of Carr's Glen shows this mill and its massive waterwheel, which lay on a north-south axis, forming a dramatic feature that cut across the valley. Ordnance Survey maps of the 1930s show the mill as unroofed and the mill pond empty. Further downstream, towards the Ballysillan Road, a farmhouse with extensive outbuildings is named as Glencarr House. A footpath is shown going up the glen, passing by the mill and extending to the Horseshoe Bend.

In 1978 much of the glen, amounting to forty acres of land, was acquired by Belfast City Council to create Carr's Glen Linear Park. By this time only a few tumbled down walls remained of the mill, which had become known locally as the Old Castle and there had been extensive dumping of wrecked cars and rubbish. Following a clean-up there was large-scale tree planting and a path network was put in place.[14] Today Carr's Glen is a valuable local park and an important gateway to access the rest of Cave Hill Country Park.

Bertie McClure

I was born and reared in North Belfast. Near where I lived was Carr's Glen and of course that was a playground for us as children, we probably played there from when we were maybe five or six. From the Ballysillan Road we would go up a lane with a very big corn field on the right. Here there were corncrakes, they craked all night, but now it's the Boys' Model School. The lane went up past McConnell's farm on the left and his farmyard was on the right, over the river. Away to the rear of the yard on the right was a single storey building, the Redpaths lived there. The girl was Minnie the boy Jim. They did not farm, they just lived there. Further up Carr's Glen was the old mill and the Craigs' house.[15]

When I was in my early teens I was walking through the glen with the dog and I called in by the Craigs' house, which is the old mill house. There were three boys there, slightly older than me. They were in short trousers, a Scouts uniform – not a complete uniform, a working uniform. They were discussing recreating the bridge, a small bridge say 150 yards from the Craigs' house over the Carr's Glen River that had got washed away. The man of the house, called Dougie, was discussing with them the possibility of cutting down trees and making a timber bridge. This seemed very interesting for a boy of my age and I spent a

Carr's Glen mill and the Craigs' house in 1954.

few days with them. We identified trees to the rear of the mill, Scots pine trees, and cut them down and shortened them accordingly. The problem was to get them from that point down to where the bridge was. So the man Dougie said go down to McConnells' farm, the first farm on the Ballysillan Road, and he loaned us a horse which no one seemed to know anything about! We were town people, not country people. But the man hooked up a trace and a cross bar and chains and showed us how to take the horse out of the yard. We set about and pulled these trees down and put them in position. They were something approaching 20 feet or 18 feet long and the bridge was strong enough to take the coal lorry. This had to have been 1952-53.

The man Dougie was very bad with his chest, blue in the face, he couldn't walk a good distance. Violet was a relative, a good bit younger than Dougie. I never could work out if Dougie owned the place or if Violet owned the place. She had a son and she went to work every day. She was a very, very small woman, a wee stocky woman, and her son's name was Ernest, Ernie Craig. Dougie was a great man with a Diana airgun, it wouldn't have been uncommon to see him shoot a blackbird to make it into soup, you know. I was appalled as a boy seeing him shooting them and you know just pulling the feathers off them. They hadn't a lot of money. I remember seeing him shoot a magpie on the back of a cow, it was picking grubs out of the back of a cow, he just knocked it over.

The mill was standing but the windows were closed with corrugated iron and ivy and the roof was missing. The house was a good house, tiled floor and two storey. Slate roof. I reckon it was a good quality house. My grandmother liked goat's milk and they kept goats so you could have went there, you didn't have to knock the door, the door was always open. You could have seen the fire, and Dougie would have come out and either milked a goat for you into a lemonade bottle or he had it sitting in a pail and poured some into a bottle. Very strong milk. The house was attached to the mill, which was just a shell, an open shell. Inside were lean-to pens for goats, he pushed them in there at night. The wheel of the mill had gone, just the pit remained with two cast iron plates for the wheel axle. Whenever I was young, the pit for the wheel seemed a terrible big depth but it may have been 10 or 15 feet. I don't know what the mill had been used for. The Craigs had not run it – they used the pit where the wheel had been for dumping rubbish.

One of the big mysteries was who owned the land further up Carr's Glen. You see, as a boy you didn't think like that, you only knew that there was a stile and a right of way. All you knew was no one chased you. There just was a walk and it was a very social thing to do in the summer time. I can picture my mother with my youngest brother in the pram, pushing it up past the Craigs' house, sitting on the grass, us playing in the river. A lot of mothers did that. Sunday it was a great courting place. You could walk as far as you like, up to the Hightown Road or across to Belfast Castle and Bellevue.

Daddystown and Mammystown

On 5 September 1840, the first wagon rolled down rails laid from a quarry on the southern slopes of Cave Hill to the coast. The wagonway ran alongside the Cavehill and Limestone Roads and three bridges were built to take the tracks under the Ballysillan, Antrim and Shore Roads. The steep gradient of the line allowed it to be operated by gravity and in the first section a cable that passed round a winding drum was attached to wagons; full wagons descending pulled up the empty wagons. The quarry operated until the 1890s when it shut, probably because there was a declining market for using the stone as ballast for sailing ships.[16]

The track of the wagonway in the 1930s. Going up the hill you could continue straight on to the quarries or take a path to the left which went to Daddystown.

Between the quarry and the upper section of Carr's Glen, along a track from the Hightown Road to the Cavehill Road, two small groups of cottages were built to house workers. These were known to all as Daddystown and Mammystown and were occupied long after the quarry became derelict. Some were used as homes, others as weekend retreats or accommodation for Scout groups. As time passed the cottages were used less often and by the early 1960s had started to become vandalised and derelict. Today the huge quarry face is still an imposing feature, though the remains of the cottages can only be traced with difficulty.

The land around the former quarry and the cottages became part of the Wallace Estate, which included a large area of heathland and upland in Ballyaghagan townland stretching from the Upper Hightown Road to the scarp around the top of Cave Hill. There were proposals for a golf course which raised concerns about the future of the area, but in 1989 Belfast City Council was able to acquire the property.[17] The Wallace Estate lands provided a connection between Carr's Glen Linear Park and the Belfast Castle Estate and today all of the area is managed as the Cave Hill Country Park. The area around the former little settlements of Daddystown and Mammystown can be explored from the Upper Hightown Road entrance to the country park.

Peggy Blair's story told by Pat Jenkins

In February 1992 Pat Jenkins talked to Peggy Blair, who had been born at Daddystown, somewhere that both Pat and her husband Jim had known in their teenage years. Pat wrote down Peggy's stories in an old school jotter and in 2006 read through her notes and gave this history of Peggy Blair.

Peggy had been born at Daddystown on 11 September 1927. There was a row of cottages at Daddystown. Sammy Clyde lived in the end cottage, the lower end. Tommy Beattie had the next one, he was a dog breeder and had the most beautiful collies. It was this house that the Sayers later got. Peggy and her family had the next two, with a communicating door. The next one was probably the Moores' cottage; Mrs Moore was Peggy's aunt. The last one was used to keep cow fodder in, though it had earlier been used by Peggy's uncles Joe and Andrew. Sammy Clyde was a Scoutmaster and he would have stayed overnight in summer time. Peggy remembered that when the Scouts came up they would sing songs, they were great company at the weekends.

Peggy's family moved out of the cottage during the war, but Peggy saw the Blitz from there, people used to call up and sleep in the house, on the floor. Mrs Moore's son-in-law used to patrol round the cottages at night, so they felt safe. She said they were very frightened, she was about 14 at the time. Peggy started working in Wolfhill and walked to and from that mill, a long walk, every day. She had to start work at 8.15am, she was up at 5.30 or 6 to get ready to go to work. If the weather was dry it was not too bad, down Carr's Glen and across the fields to the Horseshoe Bend and then on down to the Wolfhill Mill. But she got soaked to the skin when it was raining. She remembered that her grandmother travelled from Daddystown in bare feet to the Wolfhill Mill. Her uncles were half timers in the same mill, they also lived in Daddystown.

Later on the Moores only came up at weekends when the weather was good. Uncle Andy went to America and joined the Merchant Navy, her Uncle Joe went to Canada, Uncle Billy married and moved to Glengormley. Uncle Andy and his wife came home, they lived in the middle house. Peggy said that his wife was 'a bit off', meaning she was a bit disturbed. She was 'odd and a bit cross' and would have followed him, a distance behind, watching him. She was a Cookstown woman. They moved to a house off Duncairn Gardens but he was killed on the road at the Capitol Cinema on the Antrim Road.

There was nice water up the road, over a stile into a field. There was no tap, it was a spring, very pure. For ordinary washing there was water at the end of the cottage, but it was not safe for drinking. They heated water over the fire, on the crook and crane, and they baked bread on the griddle, soda farls. Ligoniel or Cavehill Road were the only shops, they had to walk a long way. They had their own cows and made their

Peggy's mother Elizabeth Blair with Darkie in 1925 or 1926.

Aunt Margaret and grandmother Elizabeth Blair with Peggy in 1929.

Peggy aged 8 pushing a pram with Rover, a Scottie dog.

own butter, but not enough to do them all week. The churn was in the next door house, there was a doorway between two of the cottages so they could go from one to the other. They had their own hens.

Peggy said it was very lonely place. One stormy night when the slates were flying, the dogs barked and the hens got very excited, Peggy's mother took a torch out but found nothing. Next morning a tramp walked out of the old shed between the hen house and byre and asked for tea and a piece. The thought of it frightened them afterwards but it didn't happen again. Sometimes someone from Mammystown came up, people called Reid lived there and some man called Brown. They weren't there very long. Later Ellie Reid lived in a cottage at the end of Hightown Road. Peggy also said that high up on the hill was Alec Hydes, who had a fierce goat. She said he was a hermit with a big long beard. Below him was a man called Semple who lived in a wee house and there was another ruined house.

Peggy lived at Daddystown until she was 15, in 1942, when they moved to a bungalow on the Hightown Road. The rent was paid to Lord Glentoran, it then became the Wallace Estate. Her Aunt Margaret had diabetes and had to give up work, and her mother had to give up her job to look after her. Peggy had to go to work alone. Peggy was married from that bungalow and moved away to Flush Road.

Roy McConnell

I was in the 29th West Belfast Scout Group and our headquarters were in Daddystown, the cottages adjacent to the quarry on the Cave Hill. We used these every weekend for all Scout activities. It was used for the Scout curriculum, testing various badges. It was a great character building exercise for us as youngsters. I would have been up there in 1950 as a Cub and then into the Scouts. We just went up first as a day person to visit the cottage, you weren't allowed to stay over, and then when I went into the Scouts the big thing was being able to stay out overnight. We would have been up there Saturdays and stayed over to Sunday and then as you got older you went up on Friday night. Our Scout Hall was in Hesketh Park, so after our troop meeting we would have walked across what was Ballysillan playing fields and up through Carr's Glen, collected the key from Violet and Dougie Craig who lived at the old mill beside the river. And then from there walked up through the trees up to the cottages. Get the fire going and have a cup of tea.

I came from the Shankill Road, the Scouts were from the Shankill Road, Crumlin Road and over at Ardyone and around Carr's Glen. A mixed group, it was before the Troubles. There would have been up to

Daddystown after a fall of snow.

20 of us staying at the cottages at the weekend. We had a small field we called the Wee Field and in that we had grass huts. Everyone had their own grass hut, we may have had 10 to 12 of these grass huts. They were made from hazels we got from down below by the river. We fastened them together and then we would have cut the grass with a sickle and formed a thatch. This was part of the test for your badge. You had to get a bucket of water and throw it over the thatch to see if it leaked. But I remember having the blankets covered in snow, the wind blowing the snow up in and onto the blankets! I remember lying under the stars in the good nights and one of my first memories of the aurora borealis, the northern lights, was lying in the wee field and watching the lights. It was a magic experience.

The Scoutmaster would have been a chap called Gerry Nevin, who was the first black belt in the north of Ireland. At that time they did judo up in front of the cottage. Billy Parker and Billy Orchin became Scout leaders and then Sam Murray. The cottage we had was fairly basic, earthen floor, a big open fireplace, cupboards, boxes for each of the patrols, an annex beside where you kept your rucksack and stuff like that. You slept upstairs in the winter or if you had a grass hut you slept there. We would feed the fire from wood from the forest. Water was from a small well going up the lane, it was renowned for its clarity. A chap called Mr Reid used to come up every year and get the water from the well to make elderberry wine. Paraffin lights – we used to get the paraffin from a house at the top of the Hightown Road.

I don't have great recollections of Mammystown, but I do remember an ex-army man who was very meticulous in his method, typical army. Old table covered in clean newspapers. He kept a goat outside for milk. He lived there. Now there were a number of cottages but I can only remember him. My memories are not very clear but I can remember a number of cottages, three or four from what I would guess. Surrounded by a small copse of trees.

Bertie McClure

I joined the 29th West Belfast Scouts and used to go up to Daddystown. It was a real paradise. All good simple activities and the people who ran it just knew how to keep young people busy. The Scouts had been going up to Daddystown since the 1930s and there was an old book that recorded their activities. You could read out what they had done years ago and nearly on the same date we would have done the same activity. One of the activities I think was called 'spotting', it was obviously based on First World War training. Daddystown was built on the side of the hill and from the first hedge you could look down to the Horseshoe Bend, down through hazel groves and swampy ground. One patrol would have half an hour or whatever to get across as far as they could towards the Horseshoe Bend. When they got there they would wave a flag and we in our patrol would wave a flag back. You needed to use binoculars. That was when the game started. The whole idea was that your team had to get up as close as possible to the observer of the team without being spotted. The 29th West Belfast Scouts followed the original scouting ideals, regenerating the activities that had been done years before. Mr Clyde would have been the driving force in that he kept the records, he had those books.

There were seven houses at Daddystown. When I was there, looking at the building, the first one on the right was the one Sam Clyde had and to the side of it was a lean-to with an earthen floor. The second was

Tommy Beattie's, the third was John Sayers' – he was a baker and at the weekend brought up stale bread and buns, stuff that he couldn't sell, which was a great bonus to us! The next house in my mind was used by the 48th Scouts, though others say that that was not right, that it was the 20th Scouts. They were sort of regarded as the opposition Scouts. Cranson and Moore had the next houses. Cranston owned a barber shop on the Oldpark and had one son called Neil. The Moore family you only saw at weekends. The last house was perhaps always empty, though I have a vague memory of a woman living there.

Scouts near Ballysillan Road heading up the hill.

The path outside of Daddystown was called the Street. It went to the Hightown Road, as you walked up the path at one point you had to cross a river – it was a concrete bridge – you turned a corner and on your right would have been a barn and an entrance to a yard. In that yard were farmyard buildings and a cottage. Certainly a family lived in that cottage and immediately backing onto that was a Victorian house, a well-kept dowdy house and two old ladies lived in that. As you continued on to where you would meet the Hightown Road there were what I think were two houses, one of which was McBurneys'. The kitchen was converted into a counter and you could buy paraffin outside, and in the house I think bread and sweets but not a big amount of provisions. Thinking back on it they were very poor. Today there is nothing left of the McBurneys' house, it stood by the Hightown Road at the corner of what is now the Council car park. Going the other way from Daddystown I just have a vague recollection of the houses further down the lane called Mammystown. People lived there, the houses were occupied. The houses were a terrace but I can't remember what they were like or how many chimneys there were; that would have been the clue to how many houses there were. I remember asking about the names, Mammystown and Daddystown. The simple answer was that that was what they were called but I never got an idea what the connection was, how they got the names.

Sam Clyde had a small bellows organ, a wee fold up organ and on Sunday morning he played the organ and everyone sang. It was a non-denominational Scout group and it was an informal thing. He very often read a poem from I think Edgar Guest or things like 'Hitch your Wagon to a Star'; it was all aimed at encouraging youth to be forward-thinking. There would not have been hymns, there would have been Scouting sort of songs. Tommy Beattie would have come in for that though later he died in an accident at Daddystown.

The 29th West Belfast Scouts were the people that could do things and someone must have said we will have a bonfire, a beacon for the Coronation of Elizabeth, on Cave Hill.[18] This was in 1953. I can remember us doing what we normally did, going and cutting stuff in the grounds of Belfast Castle. There was no one to stop us doing that, though in Scouting you were encouraged to take only failing or dead timber. So anyway, we gathered the stuff in the castle estate and built it as a bonfire and I have a recollection there were dignitaries, more up-market sort of Scouts and Scoutmasters turning up. We built the thing, there was quite a turn-out doing that, but then there was the worry someone would set it on fire before the time. I can remember there was four of us: Jerry Nevin, myself, Derek Campbell and I think his younger brother Ronnie Campbell. We slept in small bivouac tents up on Napoleon's Nose, in the hollows, and we were there whenever they lit the bonfire. Someone turned up who seemed to be in charge and they had binoculars and they kept looking across I think towards Scotland and then they lit it. The beacon was right up on McArt's Fort, by the Ordnance Survey post. It wasn't that exciting, it was just something you done. It was quite common for Scouts to sleep out on the face of the hill, where it is quite flat and heathery, in July and August. The thing you were surprised to see was that there were hundreds of shooting stars, hundreds every night.

Sam Moore

I have a number of cousins and we were very much like brothers and sisters. We were all taken to Daddystown from the time we were born, really. My first recollection of the place and the cottage my grandmother rented was during the war. We were taken up there whenever there was word of pending bombing raids in Belfast. We had been taken there and placed on a mattress on the floor and I can vaguely remember seeing my uncle silhouetted against the half door, he had the top half open. But it's a brief memory – my first memory of Daddystown. We were taken there by our grandparents or parents or aunts and uncles, you know we had a great extended family. We walked up through Carr's Glen. I did it again a couple of years ago with my son and I hadn't done it for many years and I was just astounded whenever I discovered just how long a journey it is. But we did it and of course everything had to be carried, all the food and other necessities.

Our cottage was the second in the row and my grandmother obtained the cottage in 1933, she paid one shilling and nine pence rent. It was very, very basic. There was just a stone floor, nothing on the floor, no carpet, mats or anything like that. There was a couple of settees and chairs and just inside the door on the right was a Welsh dresser where plates and cups and things were placed. And then there was a window, a beautiful little lattice window to the left. It had diamond panes of glass and under that was a table and chairs where we had our meals. There was a large open fire and all the cooking was done on that. There was a metal griddle placed directly on the fire, a wood fire. Obviously there was no electricity. There was a chaise longue – that was the most fancy part of the cottage! I think all of the furniture was part of the deal she got when she rented the cottage.

The Moore family at Daddystown around 1941-42. In the front of the picture is Cousin Beth with her mother behind and Sam Moore with Aunt Lily behind. To the right are Sam's grandmother's half sister Minnie and her husband Bob. Behind Aunt Lily is Sam's mother holding Cousin Willy in her arms and alongside her is Madge Mullan. In the back row on the left are Billy Graham and Sam's grandmother and on the right Cousin Willy's mother Marty and father Sandy.

There was just a single room, one up and one down. Upstairs there were four beds in a row across the floor and there were no curtains, no privacy. The only privacy was the ladies went up to the bedroom first, got undressed and into bed and put the light out. The men then came up and that was it. The staircase ran up at the end of the room, no banister rail, just a stairway up through the ceiling. Upstairs there was a rectangular opening without any rail around it. You had to be careful you didn't fall over there. There was a good height around the centre of the bedroom but at the side with the roof rising there you had to be careful you didn't bump your head. I can remember when we were put to bed, there

Tommy Beattie with his collies.

were times my cousin Beth and I would crawl over to the edge of the opening and pop our heads down and we were looking at the people talking downstairs, looking at them upside down. Upstairs there was a ship's lamp, an oil lamp. Downstairs there were Tilley lamps and candles and oil lamps.

My grandmother was very intuitive; she was always making sound decisions that were of great benefit to the family. She must have foreseen that by taking the cottage it would be very good for the family, and that was the way it turned out. Not only for our family but for many, many friends who also visited there. We didn't have any toys as such. We played in the stream or on a rope swing on a nearby tree, we were taken for walks over the fields and into the quarry. In the quarry we found tiny strawberries – wild strawberries about the size of a pea and they were very sweet. I remember Beth and I having to go to fetch milk, it was probably straight from the cow, not pasteurized. We walked up the lane, up to the Hightown Road, turned left down the road. We had a jug and the old lady in a farm gave us some milk and we walked back. I just passed there the other day and the house is still there but derelict at this stage.

The first cottage was unoccupied, it was used for storage and it was also used for keeping goats, it housed goats at the kidding time. The next one to ours was unoccupied as well and then the next along was occupied by the Blairs. Now the Blairs actually lived there at the time. There was Maggie, Lizzie and Lizzie's daughter Peggy. Peggy became friends with my aunts and uncles; they were round about the same age. Lizzy was a very nice lady but I think Maggie gave her a hard time, so she did. The cottages after that I can't remember how they were occupied at the start but after a while the end cottage became occupied by the 29th Scout group. The Scout leader was a man called Sam Clyde, a really remarkable person. One of the cottages was taken by a man called Tommy Beattie. Tommy always had three collie dogs whenever he arrived up at the cottages and they were always immaculately groomed.

The cottages came to an end probably around the early 1960s. It came to a point where people were breaking in. It just became too much, you know. The Blairs had left some years before. It was just very unfortunate, a very sad time. It had been a great experience for a weekend, everyone should experience that. No electricity, no running water, no central heating, no radio, television, telephone. Zero! It was living very close to nature.[19]

Jim Jenkins

George Sayers was round about my age and I used to go up to Daddystown with him and a crowd at weekends. We got together because we all played tennis at Cave Hill. George's father and some of his friends had previously used the cottage, they had not only used it at weekends, but they used to stay there for three or four weeks during summer, walk down to the Antrim Road to the Waterworks to get the tram to the middle of town to work and back up the same thing at night. They would do that for weeks, apparently. Mr Sayers had died and we rented the cottage – I think we paid half a crown a month between about six or eight of us! We did quite a bit of work on the cottage, painted the front door and put

a railing round it at the front. We would be up on a Saturday afternoon in good weather. We never stayed overnight but some of us would go up again for a walk on Sunday morning, to see who was knocking about. Talk to Tommy Beattie and his dogs.

The cottage was quite small, it was quite dark as it had only one small window at the front, there wasn't a window at the back. You went in the door and there was an entrance area, about three feet across and then there was just one room with a fireplace with a crook and a crane. The fireplace was not too big but higher than most of them are today. There was a narrow staircase but upstairs there was just a floor and it was very, very low. We went up once or twice to look but there was no point, you could not even stand up. It was perhaps used as a dormitory, you would just creep up and sleep. There was no toilet, you went into the back fields. At the front it was just stony ground, not paved. The roofs were slated.

Photograph by Jim Jenkins of friends at Daddystown in 1947. Back row from left to right are John Markwell, Desmond Rippard, Lander Ringland and Sinclair Annsley. Front row from the left are Johnny Harper and George Sayers. In the front can just be seen Ken Ross, who had been pushed as the picture was taken!

We used to take it in turns, when we were going up at weekends, to bring sausages, bread, some coal and sticks – enough to keep the fire going for a few hours – that was all we needed. I can remember, and this might surprise you, but when we started going in that cottage there was a piano. Now the piano had very few keys, it was a wreck. We made a seat out of that piano. We could never find out who had brought it up there, we used to ask Sammy Clyde where did the piano come from, but he didn't know. He had a wee harmonium. But how they got a piano up there?

We would go up and park our food and everything and then went out onto the front of the quarry where there was a flat part and we played quoits. The quoits were quite heavy metal rings, about six inches

Track of the old wagonway photographed in the early 1930s from the bridge over the Ballysillan Road. In the distance can be seen the wall that formed the southern boundary to the wooded Belfast Castle Estate. Today the bridge has gone and the path, recalled by Jim Jenkins as a white lane called the Lines, is the Upper Cavehill Road.

across. We were told they had been made in the shipyard and apparently had been used by Mr Sayers senior and his mates. We would throw the quoits and try to get them over a metal peg. There was an area there we called the Knowes, in front of the quarry, small hills where the quarry waste had been dumped. We didn't get up to a lot because we weren't there that long. I mean we would go up in the afternoon and fouter about, get the fire going and one thing and another and then go out and play quoits, go back to the cottage and have something to eat. This would have been a Saturday, so Saturday night we were always going to a dance. Either the Floral Hall or the tennis club.

We had the cottage next to Sammy Clyde and the next one was empty. The Blair family had gone, the only other person I remember was an elderly woman who lived at one of the other cottages. She would not have spoken to us at all or you know looked near you or anything. And I used to see her an odd time walking down the Limestone Road but that's all, I knew nothing about her. She was an odd looking person and fairly elderly. That would have been around 1941. I still would have been going up until I was married, that was 1949. After that the boys would have still been going up but by then I don't think there was anyone living there, the houses were just used occasionally.

As far as I know Daddystown was given its name because this was where the men who had originally worked in the old quarry were billeted at night – I think it was a sort of dormitory. I had been told that they were Paddies, they may have been men from the south. Mammystown may have been where the wives of some of the men lived. Mammystown was gone by my time and I knew nothing about it, just the name.

There was once a railway for transporting the stone from the quarry right down to the harbour; a double-arched bridge carried the Ballysillan Road over the lines. Going up from the bridge the old railway was a white lane that led through a farmyard and past two cottages owned by people called Hydes and Spratt. Further up the hill the lane divided, to the left led to Daddystown and straight on took you to the quarry. At the junction where the two paths met there was a house where people called Falls lived and behind this house was Norah's Grave, where two young lovers had committed suicide. I remember Norah's Grave was marked by white stones, though these disappeared. The railway is gone a long time but if you went up the Cavehill Road and straight up to the quarry,

Former bridge at the Ballysillan Road.

that was always known by all the locals as the Lines. If I went up over the Cave Hill my father would say, 'What way did you go, up the Lines or did you go up the side of the trees?' When I was in my teens, there was one particular place where you could still see the lines, the metal railway line, just a short section. The wall of the Belfast Castle Estate was on the right when you went up the lines. The wall was pretty well continuous up to the quarry. Where it was very steep the wall stopped and there was the black palings. The black palings was a high fence, around about 30 feet long, 7-8 feet high, a good wee bit above head height. Made of timber, painted black. It was the boundary of the castle estate. The fence is long gone, bits kicked down or taken for firewood.[20]

Belfast Castle Estate

Some of the oldest surviving records for Cave Hill, dating from the early 1700s, refer to the development of a deer park. This was enclosed with stone walls and wooden fencing (paling) and managed by a uniformed park keeper who lived on the hill in a thatched house. The park was created by the Donegall family, who had extensive landholdings in south Antrim. Although the Donegalls were absentee landlords living in England during much of the 18th century, the park was kept stocked with deer[21] and according to one all too brief newspaper article of 1790, the family also built a temporary house somewhere on Cave Hill. This was perhaps a rustic structure where, during one of their trips to Belfast, they could take in the view of their deer and their extensive estate lands.[22]

The Cave Hill Deer Park contained a herd of deer until 1859, when they were sold by the 3rd Marquis of Donegall, who had plans to develop a new mansion house at this prominent and historic site. By the late 1860s construction of this house, which became known as Belfast Castle, had commenced and it was completed by 1871. The Marquis also built a stable block on land acquired just to the north of the castle, a gate lodge on the Antrim Road and, on a rocky prominence overlooking the Antrim Road, the Chapel of the Resurrection. The chapel was the first building to be completed and was dedicated to the memory of his son and also housed the remains of family members that he had transported from the vaults at St. Nicholas' Church at Carrickfergus. While work progressed on these buildings, the planting began of thousands of trees in the surrounding land to create the woods that today clothe the hill slopes.[23]

In the 1880s, the Belfast Castle grounds were expanded by the acquisition of Martlett Towers, a property to the north of the castle which had a large house together with outbuildings and walled garden. These buildings were adapted for use as part of the castle estate and subsequently some additional houses were constructed in the castle grounds, including a gamekeeper's cottage in the woods on the hill and, on the Antrim Road, a post office/gate lodge and a terrace known as Martlett Cottages or Martlett Row.[24]

The 3rd Marquis of Donegall must have seen his project to build Belfast Castle and the Chapel of the Resurrection complete with its new ancestral vault as an everlasting memorial to the family and its role in the development of Belfast. However, the castle was probably the last of the really grand houses set in extensive landscaped grounds to be built in Belfast and it had only a fleeting role as a family home. Remarkably, the death notices of the 3rd Marquis of Donegall in 1883 reveal that although he had commissioned the building of the castle on Cave Hill, he had been an absentee landlord and had never visited the mansion.[25] His daughter Harriett (who became the Countess of Shaftesbury) inherited the property and is reported to have spent some months each year at Belfast Castle and her son, the 9th Earl of Shaftesbury, was, for a time, resident. However by the end of the

1920s, less than 60 years after the castle had been built, it was unoccupied and during the Depression attempts had to be made to find a new use for the site.[26] The lower slopes near the Antrim Road, including ground around the gate lodge and the Chapel of the Resurrection, were sold for housing and to provide land for Belfast Royal Academy. In 1934 the mansion and the remaining lands were acquired by Belfast Corporation for a public park.[27]

After acquisition by the Corporation, the castle, its associated buildings and the extensive grounds were managed by the Tramways Committee as an adjunct to the gardens, zoo and amusements that this committee ran at Bellevue and Hazelwood. Belfast Castle became a popular venue for functions, though proposals for popular attractions for the castle grounds put forward by the Tramways Committee raised concerns.[28] It was perhaps fortunate that all plans for development were put on hold during the Second World War when the castle and some outbuildings were requisitioned, initially for use by the Royal Air Force and subsequently by the Admiralty.[29]

In the post war years the Tramways Committee had a growing budget deficit and there was a lack of investment in the castle estate. Martlett Towers became disused and, after being set on fire by vandals, was demolished. In 1962, the Parks and Cemeteries Committee took over management of the Belfast Castle Estate together with the zoo and Hazelwood. However the problem of funding remained and by 1969 Belfast Corporation was proposing to lease the castle as a hotel. This plan generated considerable public opposition and was abandoned following a public inquiry.[30] At this time there was a contract for catering at the castle but when this ended in 1971, it was not renewed and the only use made of the building was for occasional parties and meetings.[31] The upper floors became dilapidated and unoccupied, with the exception of a caretaker's residence and a room used by the zoo to quarantine tropical birds.[32]

Eventually, in the late 1970s, a refurbishment programme started with financial support from central government and the castle reopened for public use in 1988.[33] Around the same time the wooded castle grounds together with the surrounding public lands at Carr's Glen, Hazelwood and the uplands on Cave Hill were integrated to form Cave Hill Country Park.[34] Today the castle is one of the city's best known landmarks, a magnificent public venue and a great place to start to explore the surrounding landscape.

Belfast Castle

Cathleen Arthurs

I can remember when I was about seven or eight, maybe younger, some woman was staying next door with close friends in the terrace where I lived, opposite the Waterworks, and we went for a walk. Anyway we found ourselves in the castle grounds and that was at the time when it was illegal, you were not allowed to be there. And that was my first impression I ever had of masses of bluebells. A whole sheet of bluebells and that was absolutely lovely. Of course we were trespassing. Bundles of bluebells in our arms, you know. I don't remember how we would have got in – I think we must have gone up round the hill – I really can't remember. I have this vivid memory of a big wall, a big stone wall, well it ran from the gate lodge at the entrance to the castle estate right up the Antrim Road, oh, I don't know how far. There were no houses on this side of the Antrim Road, just woods and that was where I saw the bluebells. That would have been in the 1920s sometime.

I was at the opening of Belfast Castle when it was taken over by the Corporation, that was in the 1930s. We were living further up the Antrim Road by that time, the corner of Salisbury. Some friends and myself went up to that. It was like a fair day with stalls and things like that. I was often at the castle after that. You used to be able to go into the castle and have afternoon tea. Certainly on Sundays you could go up.

In my teenage times we used to go to, as we called them in those days, 'hops' on a Saturday night. This was in the 1930s. There was always a band – none of this disco nonsense – just dancing, you know. You didn't really dress up for it, it was just casual. A lot of the lads came from playing rugby or football. Hops were all the thing in my day. And then I remember also around about the same period going to dress dances up there and one of the things that always struck me was that there was no bar and the décor was pretty grim, really, when you look back on it. The boys would go down, they had to go down to the cellars for drink. The cellars did not look anything like the cellars look now. They were just rooms with cheap wallpaper on them. Whoever you were with would say did you want a drink and I would have gone down with them to the cellars. The tables were those collapsible card tables and paper tablecloths and this awful cheap wallpaper. And you had to go out of the room to this secret bar – well, it wasn't secret – they wouldn't have been doing it if it hadn't been licensed, but it was such a desperate way, you know, at a dress dance to be having to get a drink. You felt as if it was like – what do you call it in America – prohibition!

But it was good craic. The dancing was good. There was a wee fellow, he used to be a tram conductor – we knew all the tram conductors going up and down the Antrim Road and they brought him in to be MC and look after the dancing in the dress dances. And they had him dressed up in tails, evening tails, black with a stiff white shirt, and the tails were so long on him they were hitting his ankles nearly, which was quite funny. And then he would make an announcement, in a classy accent he would say 'the next dance will be a heads to tails dance!' That lot went off and that lot stayed on. Funny times. It was this sort of trying to be awfully good. This half be heads and this tails. Oh God, we used to stand up and clap!

Jean Martin

I grew up at Broomhill Park and went to school at Richmond Lodge and when I left school at 18, in June, I went straight into the Wrens. That was 1942. I suppose I must have known someone who worked in the Plot up at Belfast Castle, but anyway, it seemed to be the most interesting place to go. So when we joined up we had to do I think three weeks in just our ordinary clothes, plain clothes, we didn't have any uniform, and at the castle I was first a messenger. This was a very good idea because you took signals and information and what not, nothing very important probably, from one office to another so you learnt your way about the castle and then I had an interview with Anne Rogers – I can't remember what her official title was. If she thought you were suitable, you got your uniform. Anyway, I wanted to go into the Plot – this was what we called the Operations Room – but there wasn't any vacancy in the Plot at the time so I was put into coding, in the Coding Office at the castle, which I absolutely hated and was absolutely hopeless at! It was so boring, just little sections of numbers, I didn't know what it meant really. Happily, I was only there for a short time and a vacancy came up at the Plot.

The Coding Office was led by I think a Petty Officer Wren, anyway it was a girl I knew, she had been at the same

Jean Martin in her Wren uniform at home with Rusty.

school as me, but she was older than I was. Then there was the Cipher Office which was run entirely by Wren officers and that was all very secret. They had a little hatch into the Plot and we put signals through, took signals back, that sort of thing.

We were in contact with the Coastguards and we got a lot of information about the movement of shipping from the RAF outside of Derry, from the radar places there. We plotted the convoys from the Clyde down out past Rathlin out to the Atlantic and we plotted convoys down from the Clyde, right down through the Irish Sea to the south, to Milford Haven, though we didn't actually go as far as Milford Haven. We plotted the Queen Mary from the Clyde out to the Atlantic and coming in again, she was a troop ship in those days. She came in of course very, very fast, I mean you hardly had time to see her before she had gone. We also plotted the coasters, there were lots of them, oh, going down from the Clyde, going from Whitehaven, out from Larne, Derry. They were quite hard to see, quite hard for the radar people to see because they were so small. Belfast was a big base for escort groups, frigates, and we certainly did plot them in and out. They would go out to meet the convoys and escort them out into the Atlantic. The Daffodil – HMS Daffodil – she plied backwards and forwards with troops between Larne and Stranraer and I gather she was a terrible old tub!

I was in the Wrens but not on duty at the time when a cruiser, the Curacao, which I think must have come down from the Clyde, because she wasn't based in Belfast, I am pretty certain. Anyway she went out to meet the Queen Mary, to escort her up the Clyde, and the Queen Mary – she always came outside of Rathlin – the Queen Mary came in and she just sliced through the Curacao. We actually knew two of the boys on that ship. There was obviously a mix-up in signals or something though they never really got to the bottom of it. It was terrible.

In the Plot there was what we called the U-Boat Situation, which was a great big map which was up on the wall and while we could see it we had nothing to do with it. There was always a Wren officer on duty and she got what we called the U-Boat Situation and she pinpointed where they were with drawing pins. I remember one night there was great panic. The Second Officer who was on duty, her husband was on a destroyer – I think it was the Oribi – and she could see that it was coming very close to these U-Boats. She was in a bit of a panic.

In the middle of the room was a big table with a map on it of all our area, the Irish Sea, and little wooden boats that we pushed according to where the convoys were. As far as I can remember they had little flags on them. It is awfully hard to remember all the details. The convoys all had code names and the big ships all had code names too.

We had Perspex sheets I think you would call them, three of them perhaps. These were marked out in a grid and we plotted the route of ships with wax pens. We were in communication with the radar stations and there was teleprinter communications with Greenock on the Clyde and the Liver Building in Liverpool and I am not absolutely certain, perhaps also with Milford Haven. There was a radio telephone link with the Orkneys, but it practically never worked. Visual signallers sent and received signals with boats in Belfast Lough. One of my best friends at the castle was a visual signaller, but you weren't supposed to talk about your work, I didn't know what she did.

In the Operations Room there were also offices behind a glass screen for the top people in the three divisions. These were the Staff Officer Convoys, our boss who was Staff Officer Plot and Staff Officer Operations. There were always one, if not two, sub-lieutenants also working in the Plot with us, though quite what they did I am not sure, they had their own little desks. The Plot was slightly L-shaped, because while at one angle we could see the three officers, you couldn't have seen them from the side. A Wren who was secretary to the Staff Officer Operations or perhaps to all the officers had a desk in the bay window overlooking the gardens, she could see out. The Plot had a high ceiling and big windows overlooking the garden that were closed with shutters at night.

All I can remember really about when we went on duty is that we were picked up by bus when we came on duty – it was not thought safe for us girls to walk up to the castle – and taken to Belfast Castle then taken back into town and then we made our own way where we wanted to go. I don't remember barbed wire or sentries. We were taken up, went in then we came out to the bus and off we went. We all wore naval uniform. The ratings uniform was a serge, navy blue skirt, white blouse and black tie and if you were a Leading Wren you had an anchor on the arm. We wore a hat just like a sailor's hat, with a ribbon, but of course it had just HMS. For security reasons you didn't have the name of a ship, though we were based in HMS Caroline, which is still down there in the docks. The officers' uniform was very attractive. Officers also had a navy blue uniform, though it was much nicer material, you know, smooth, and they wore a tricorn hat, three-pointed, very attractive, with a naval badge on it.

In the basement there was a canteen, though I only remember eating there about twice. The switchboard was also in the basement. Cipher Office, Coding Office, Signals Office and Operations Room were on the one floor – I think this was the ground floor. I think, I think the Chief Petty Officer, known to us all as Chiefy – a very nice man – his office was on that floor too and the head Wren, Anne Rogers, had an office there, in on the right when you went in. Upstairs were rooms for officers, for Admiral King and Lord Kilmorey, Captain Lord Kilmorey. Although I never slept in the castle I can remember that there was a dormitory, I remember going into it. I think that might have been on the second floor. There were also some civilians in offices right at the top of the building. That's my picture of it, I can't exactly tell you how it was, that's just

View from Cave Hill taken around the late 1930s. The castle forms an imposing feature and on the far right the Chapel of the Resurrection can be glimpsed within a patch of woodland. The Belfast Castle Estate grounds used to extend down to the Antrim Road but by the time this picture was taken housing had started to creep up the hill.

as far as I can remember, it's a long, long time ago. Immediately after the war I can remember going to a private dance at the castle, when all the young men came back; we had all missed out on our 21st birthday parties so there was an awful number of private dances. I suppose the dance must have been where the Plot was, it was sort of a long room. You see all these partitions would have been taken down, taken away.

We were terribly lucky, I can only remember doing drill twice in the years I was in the Wrens. I don't remember doing any saluting except the odd time we would have been invited onto a ship. When anybody you knew was lost that was terrible. One frigate that I was taken onboard for drinks was sunk just about a week later. Those were awful things but by and large it was all a bit of a lark, really, you know. At 19 you don't take anything terribly seriously unless it affects you personally, you know.[35]

Jim Jenkins

In the years after the war, at Belfast Castle there were dances on Saturday, but nothing much else happened there. There were dances at both the castle and Floral Hall. The general idea was that boys went maybe with their mates to the Floral Hall and girls went with their friends but once you started going steady with somebody, you went to the castle. Very few went to the castle without a partner. Well then the castle was also used, for instance, by organisations like Instonians or firms or associations who would once a year hire it for a dance. The dance hall is not that big and I don't remember anything happening in the basements or upper rooms. There was no drink or meals. The hall and staircase were lined with stuffed heads, real heads of animals that had been shot, things like lions and bears.[36] It was ballroom dancing at the castle, it was formal dress, certainly you would have had a tie – shirt and tie. The staff wore uniforms. People were well-behaved in those days, the peak of misbehaviour was throwing streamers over the stuffed animal heads or putting a cigarette in their mouths! You didn't get up to the sort of tricks people get up to nowadays.

Craig Wallace

In the 1960s, in my predecessors' time, Hastings had the franchise of the castle. It was mainly a restaurant and a place for weddings. I remember going to a wedding there in 1963, a very pleasant place but you only saw the reception rooms – the big ballroom was used as the place for dining. Of course they weren't responsible for the structure of the castle and the castle was in a very bad state of repair. Hastings gave up the franchise, I think about 1971,[37] and when I started as director of parks the former director, Reginald Wesley, left me with the words that there was no use for the castle, and he was leaving that problem for me! The castle was very badly run down, I used to say that pigeons were flying in and out of the windows. I was also told that the painters in the Parks Department threatened to go on strike because they had been instructed to paint the doors white. You know many of the doors were pitch pine and they threatened to go on strike – they were going to destroy these doors with white paint! This was before my time. It would have been a desecration.

The renovations started in 1978 or thereabouts. It was very expensive work though there was grant aid. It was reopened for use in November 1988, just two months after I had retired. There was a luncheon in the castle to celebrate the reopening. I remember one councillor saying, in the castle, that the renovations were a complete waste of money, but what were people like that going to do? Allow the place to crumble into disrepair? It was in a very bad state, no doubt about it. The architect concerned took a great interest in the project. There was a most strange system of water supply which I can't really detail but there was a reservoir further up the Cave Hill and the water flowed down to the castle and was stored, I think, in a tank way up in the rafters which was a sort of medieval form of water supply but that changed, of course. There was a chapel – a small chapel in the basement – a private chapel for the Shaftesburys. You would have realised going into it that it wasn't just another room.

The lookout at the castle tower.

If you are standing in front of the castle, on the right hand side of the building, way up there, you will find you can get onto a platform, a wooden landing for want of a better term. Now I am bad at heights but I remember taking the Parks Committee up there. Now we walked through a door onto this outside landing which had obviously been built on. Wooden flooring, you could see through the gaps onto the ground many feet below. And that was used as a look-out over the lough by the Royal Navy, you see the castle was headquarters of the Navy in Northern Ireland during the war. One of the rooms way at the top, again as I say on the right-hand side, you will find that you can get onto this wooden landing. And that window is still there. I am terrible for heights, I didn't like it at all! But anyway, that is where it is.

Well, Dennis Waring, the Assistant Director of Parks, went up to the castle one morning. This was before the renovations were carried out, and the overnight watchman was standing outside with his dog and he mentioned to Dennis that he would never go into the castle again. He was lodged during the night in one of the upstairs rooms, way at the top, and the dog suddenly gave a loud yelp, the hair stood up on its back, you see, and it flew under the table. And things I am told started to move, the table started to move about and the man had this very frightening sensation. He and the dog left the castle in the middle of the night and Dennis Waring found them in the morning outside, vowing never to go back in again. Now, whether there was a ghost or presence or whatever, I don't know, but that was the story about the ghost. Now Dennis pooh-poohed the story but I was more sympathetic.

Did you know I obtained a painting for the castle of the second Marquis of Donegall? A curator of local history at the Ulster Museum phoned me up one day, there was going to be a painting of the Marquis of Donegall auctioned in London, it was not in great condition and shouldn't be too expensive. I got permission from the committee to bid for it and it was purchased for a relatively small sum, from memory around £2,000, something like that. And we acquired this big oil painting and got it restored and this is why it is hanging in the castle today. You will find my report and details in the minutes, it was in the 1980s.

Alan Jones

There were three attendants in the estate when I started to work as foreman. They did jobs like litter picking, opening and closing gates, checking on vandalism and anti-social behaviour and working along with the grounds teams carrying out maintenance. One of the attendants had the accommodation which was up at the far top northeast corner of the castle, over the kitchens. Now during the period he was here, there would have been functions and the attendants would have worked the doors. People were able to hire out the castle, bring in their own caterers, hold weddings or functions, whatever you liked. Usually just the main function room and the ground floor level. There were times when for company events for some big promotion they would have taken the whole castle over, they would have used practically every room fit for use and would have had flags up the flagpole. You could have hired the whole castle for I think it was £120 for a night!

Tommy Maxwell was the name of the guy who was the attendant living in the building. He was woken one night by crackling and banging and when he went down he realised there was a fire in the main hall and the flames were coming up into the second floor.[38] He got fire extinguishers and a hose and he kept the flames at bay until the fire brigade got here. And the fire brigade actually said that if the doors into the function room hadn't been closed we would have lost the building. Tommy was able to keep the flames back from going onto the second floor. At that particular time the Council had been looking at restoring the whole building and bringing in more modern facilities. It was very basic: there was no restaurant, no coffee shop, curtains and carpets full of holes, in tatters, so it was closed and renovated. Tommy and his wife Margaret, she was a part-time cleaner at the castle, they retired around the time that the castle was renovated and they moved out.

I remember there was an old bear's head that used to hang over the fireplace near the entrance. The park manager's office was the room that is now reception at the main entrance to the castle. There is a big

metal door in the basement café, it was at one time a walk-in safe. I was in there, we had a key for it. There was a place that had been a chapel, in the basement, just below the reception room at the entrance. It had to go when they put in the lift, part of it was where the lift is now. There were two rooms with small stained glass windows, nothing else, nothing religious. It must have been there since the castle was a private house. There were two ways into the chapel, an entrance from the garden and a door from within the building at the bottom of the stone spiral staircase.

The cannons in front of the castle – well, when Beechvale Nursery was opened up, the growing of bedding plants was transferred from Ormeau to Beechvale, that left Ormeau Yard more or less derelict. They cleared the greenhouses at Ormeau and they were levelling it out when they came across one of the cannons. And after they brought someone out and had a look they found a second, they were dug up and they found two altogether. This would have been in the late 1970s. They were cleaned up and painted and eventually brought up to the castle when they renovated the place. There are three here now, but I am near one hundred percent certain that there were two found at Ormeau. I think one came from somewhere else.[39]

Brendan Toland

I was at the castle on only two occasions prior to taking up employment with Belfast City Council which was in 1994. I remember starting in the Cecil Ward Building in the city centre that day and I was driven up here to the castle by the head of parks, at that time Maurice Parkinson, and on the way up thinking I just could not believe how lucky I was to become manager of such an iconic building in Belfast. Absolutely magnificent views over the city. With my background in hospitality I was thinking to myself what a wonderful place it would be for all kinds of events.

Now we have 200-300 weddings here every year and Belfast Castle is the most popular venue for civil weddings in Northern Ireland – the law changed in 2004 to allow people to get married in places like the castle. It is popular because of its location, beautiful photographic opportunities and wonderful views over the city. Also the elegant staircase which no bride can resist descending into the wedding room. Weddings generally run from about Easter through to the end of October. We could be doing seven, eight, nine, ten weddings a week. Then there are conferences and the restaurant, which is open seven days a week and the visitor centre which draws a huge number of people. Out the back is the Adventurous Playground, the waymarked walks and the hill. So all in all it makes for a very pleasant visitor experience.

The stone staircase linking the castle ballroom with the garden. One stone is carved with the date 1894, though it is not known who designed this magnificent structure.

On our tours we get a lot of Women's Institute ladies, guilds, and often some of the ladies were actually based here working for the Royal Navy during the Second World War or remember just being in the castle or its environs in the 40s and 50s. A number of brides or grooms who come here to be married have mothers and fathers who had marriage receptions here 30, 40, 50 years ago. We hear a lot of those stories. Then we sometimes get babies' christenings, First Communion and Confirmation lunches. Some use the restaurant to celebrate their engagement and then maybe have their wedding service here as well. The castle is open 364 days of the year, you can come into it anytime to just look around the visitor centre or look at the rooms. You can go into the cellar area where you can visit the antique shop or have a cup of coffee, lunch or dinner. It's open all the time, no one is excluded. The arrival of the cruise ships in Belfast as well has had a big impact on us. When the visitors from the cruise ships are out around the city, invariably they will arrive at the castle. On any given day we can have 12, 14, 16 coaches arrive. It is lovely to see people from all over the world. Traditionally around Easter is a time when a lot of people come up round the castle and visit Cave Hill Country Park. Easter Monday and Easter Tuesday are also very popular days for weddings.

The castle estate is the heart and soul of Cave Hill Country Park with the castle at its core and we decided to apply for the Green Flag Award because we felt it was well worthy of the badge of excellence that the Green Flag would give it. A lot of hard work went into getting the Green Flag but when we had the assessors over from England in 2009 I was so proud when we brought them round. You could see that they were absolutely overwhelmed with the facilities we have, the standard which is kept, how welcoming the park is, how well integrated everything is. We were lucky enough to achieve the Green Flag standard – we were the first Council park to achieve Green Flag status.

We had a letter from Lord Donegall just last week, asking a few questions about the castle. Just like all the correspondence from the family, he just signed the letter 'Donegall'. The family still has an association with Saint Nicolas' Church in Carrickfergus and they would attend functions there, and when they do they tend to come in here. The last time Lord Donegall came in here you know he was just very casually dressed in his Aran sweater, holes in the elbows but very much lord of the manor still. They are always absolutely thrilled that the castle is maintained so well. The gardens too are absolutely beautiful. They are appreciative and we obviously owe them, the Donegalls, a debt for the legacy that they have left behind.

The Chapel of the Resurrection with Belfast Castle and Cave Hill in the distance. This picture probably dates from around 1900. Today the chapel is unused and is surrounded by housing, and can only be glimpsed behind gardens along Innisfayle Park.

Chapel of the Resurrection

Heather Marion Swan

The Church of Ireland, Saint Peter's, took over the Chapel of the Resurrection in the estate grounds. I was the first child christened there after the Shaftesburys had left. I was christened in 1938. It was a lovely wee small church. Our youth choir belonging to Saint Peter's used to sing there on a Sunday afternoon at three o'clock. There were services from, I would say, April to the end of October. After that it got too cold and though they had a big boiler down below that you lit and all, it didn't heat it that well. There were still coffins of the Donegalls there in the crypt but they were removed because they were vandalised.

There was a pet's graveyard with wee headstones by the church with the names of dogs belonging to the estate. I don't remember just where they are, I haven't been up there for years. It was a lovely chapel and a chap who is dead and gone, Robert, used to play the organ there, a wee organ you had to pump; some days it sounded good and some days it didn't. It wouldn't have taken more than about 50 people. It was small, really small, but very homely. We all loved going there. It used to be very, very popular for small weddings.

The ornate interior of the chapel.

The gamekeeper and his cottage

Winnie Arbuthnot

The Armstrongs lived up on the hill until the late 1940s or 50s. He was the gamekeeper and ran around with a gun, around the estate.[40] Running around doing nothing with a gun under his arm frightening everybody, you know. Everybody was afraid of him. You would have seen him, see there was a fence near our house, a wire fence up to the wooden gates and we used to be through the hole in the fence.

We called him old Da' Armstrong. He thought he owned the place, he wouldn't have let a crow light as we used to say. We used to be up through a hole in the wire fence and you ran if you saw him coming. A big tall man, a big tummy, plus fours and a Harris tweed coat. Always with a dog, a spaniel sort of dog. His son worked as a ranger in Bellevue. They were hermits, really, way up there. No one ever seen them, I never saw Mrs Armstrong in my life. They were up at the back of the castle, up on the hill. I don't remember anyone else living up there, it was an awful place to live, coming in the dark at night, no lights, no nothing. I don't know how they ever lived there.

Heather Marion Swan

My grandmother, Julia Armstrong, who ran the Cavehill Post Office, had a relative, Sammy Armstrong, who was gamekeeper for the Belfast Castle Estate. I think Julia and Sammy were cousins. Sammy Armstrong's house was above the castle. As you come up to the castle you see a little place where people park and you will see a path going up, S-shaped, and you followed it up and it would have been near where the old reservoir was – just in there. There was one main room, two bedrooms off that room and a kitchen. There was no bathroom or anything, that was it. There was no electric going up to Uncle Sammy's and Auntie Annie's, oil went up once a month and turf and wood, it went on a donkey and cart. It was steep, quite a steep journey. Sammy was married to Annie and they had two children, Maudy and Percy. Before coming to work at the Belfast Castle Estate they had lived at Dungiven. We have an old postcard which gives their address as Eden Lodge, Dungiven. Sammy was always a gamekeeper but when he came to work at Cave Hill, that's a mystery to me. He had a ruddy red face, about six foot, broad, very broad and a wee bit like Billy Bunter. Loved to talk, loved his pipe, loved his shooting. He

Mr Armstrong the gamekeeper.

wore tweeds, plus fours, knitted socks. And he would walk down every day with the dog to get the paper from mummy and daddy and have a cup of tea and walk on up again. He only had a gun with him if he was going out shooting. He left there when they were getting on in years, I would say when they were nearly 80. They went to live in Middlesbrough with their daughter. That was when the Scouts took over the house. I am sure he started working there when it was a private estate owned by the Shaftesburys. When I was a child and the estate had become a park he was still working, as far as I know he then was in charge of the park rangers who looked after the hill. We used to go up in the dark to their house to play cards on a Saturday and Sunday, that would have been with my parents. We would all go up to Uncle Sammy's. I always remember going during the Second World War when the military was in the castle, they would shout, 'Who goes there?' and having a gun and all that sort of thing.

Harry Porter

North Belfast District Scouts covered an area from Glengormley down to the Shore Road Metropolitan Tabernacle, to the bottom of Cliftonville Road, up the Oldpark Road to the top of the Ballysillan. There would have been about 15 Scout groups in that area, which made up a Scout district. They were the ones who rented this cottage in the Belfast Castle Estate as a weekend cottage for Scouts. Boys used it for weekend camps in the mid to late 1950s. There was a kitchen at the back but no spring locally, you had to go a couple of hundred yards down to the main path where there was a spring – that was your water supply. We didn't have it for very many years before vandals set fire to it. The roof was felt and even though there were steel shutters on the windows somebody obviously managed to break in and set fire to the place.[41]

It's difficult to describe where the cottage was because paths that were walkable are now virtually impassable. It was maybe 150 yards south of an old reservoir on the hill, a deep concrete reservoir built to provide water in case of fire at the castle. One way to the cottage was to follow the track from the fire reservoir on the hill, down the short steep slope. But if I remember rightly the main path from the cottage went straight down the hill onto the main path that goes across the hill. An outcrop of limestone rock which, if anyone remembers, used to be daubed on a regular basis with black magic symbols years ago – it was painted over by the Council but the symbols reappeared – looking at the hill the cottage was just to the left of that outcrop.

Scouts at the gamekeeper's cottage in the woods above Belfast Castle.

Before the Scouts used the building it had been a gamekeeper's cottage. That's what we were told. Also I have been told that there were two gamekeepers in two cottages and that one of the last gamekeepers was James Greer. His son, Gerry Greer, who now lives in Scotland, was one of the assistant Scout leaders with the 76th Scout Group. He told us that it had been his father's house. I don't know where the other gamekeeper's house was but my guess is that it is the ruined cottage over towards the Cavehill Road, in the woods by the path that goes across the hill towards the limestone quarries. Gerry Greer was absolutely adamant that his father had been a gamekeeper for the Castle Estate and that there had been two gamekeepers.[42] Gerry was born in 1928 and he said he did not live in the gamekeeper's cottage, his father had left before that, but he always remembered the gamekeeper's gun sitting in the corner of the new house, it sat there for years. He also said there was a photograph of his father in front of the gamekeeper's cottage with his shotgun. He had a very clear memory of all this. He was also very clear that it wasn't just gamekeeping that they did, they planted trees and looked after vegetables in the walled garden.

Originally the main entrance to the estate, today the gates have gone but the lodge has survived.

The Antrim Road gate lodge

Margaret Redpath

It was only after my mother bought the gate house that she said that when she was walking past it my father would say, 'I would have loved to have that wee place, to buy it or live in it.' I think my mum – her name was Catherine Colgan – bought it in '79 and lived in it for about 10 years. My parents were just working class people and rented a little terraced house and then they bought a house when I was in my teens. So with the proceeds of that after my father died my mother bought the gate lodge. It had been lying empty, I don't know who had owned it previously. She decided she would like it and set about acquiring it. And she got it quite cheaply I think because it only had one cold tap and an outside loo at that time.

She moved into it the way it was, basically it has two downstairs rooms. It has a lovely porch around the back which is supported by a sandstone pillar. A nice sitting room where the little round bay is and it has another window at the back, so it is a lovely light room, a very high ceiling. And then a main living room which goes from the front to the back that has a curving staircase that goes upstairs. Red and black tiled floor. The sitting room has a lovely fireplace with a stone surround, I don't know whether it was slate or marble, I think it had been painted.

The main living room had a fireplace in the corner at an angle and I think it had been a range at one time though when my mother bought the house it had a wee Devon fireplace. During the course of the work she got that all taken out and there was a huge hole that she had to have filled and she got a builder to build a red brick fireplace; not particularly in keeping with the house but better than what had been there before. She did it on a shoestring. There was a little galley scullery with just a sink and cold tap and a yard. There were two bedrooms upstairs and I suspect there had only been one as there was a wooden partition, not a robust partition, but it made a double bedroom and single bedroom. There was no decoration to speak of, it was really quite run down, shabby. Basically it was a two up, two down.

My mother got plans drawn up and was able to make a kitchen, bathroom and a single bedroom with a built-in wardrobe in the yard area. She knocked down the old scullery. She put in central heating and opened up the stairs which I think had been sheeted in. She decided it would be safer and better to have a side entrance and went through the process, got planning permission and had a gap made in the hedge and put a gate on. A very keen gardener and the garden was all overgrown. I did some of the heavy work for her, dug out bushes and stuff like that. My mother created a lovely garden, she loved her garden. Had a garage built and paved a lovely area, it looks quite nice, I drive past quite

Gargoyle at the gate lodge.

often. Set about decorating it, various members of the family helped. Her brother did the wallpapering in the tall big sitting room which was quite a feat. I helped with the painting and my husband did the outside.

She took a great deal of trouble: she got paint that exactly matched the terracotta ridge tiles to paint the downspouts. She also got the outside of the house renovated and got the pillar at the porch rebuilt, it had worn away. She got help from Historic Buildings, a grant towards the cost. There was quite a bit of damp but she got that sorted out. All the old spouting and the gargoyle by the rain spout had to be cleaned up. She found a little bit of the old cast iron gate, the gate for the little round-topped entrance in the wall. It was lying in the garden so she got a new one made – it was only wrought iron, not as heavy, but she incorporated the design into it. My mother loved living there, you know. Just her little paradise.

She actually got a letter from Historic Buildings congratulating her on how sensitively she had restored the gate lodge. You know, restored it to what it should have looked like, which pleased her. After she died unfortunately it was empty for quite a while. There was vandalism. I myself became quite good at glazing, putting in windows; they used to just break the window and climb in. They didn't do any permanent harm but made a bit of a mess. Eventually we got it sold, to the dentist. He put up the little metal grids on the windows for security, they were not there when my mother lived there. Diamond shaped, I don't think they are obtrusive or out of keeping. The dentist told me I was welcome to come round, to have a look now it's a surgery, but I actually have never been.

The Shaftesbury children's playhouse

Irene Bell

There was some place, and I'm not 100 percent sure where about it was in the castle estate, a children's playhouse for the Shaftesbury children when they were growing up. It was just like a summerhouse. Beautifully furnished inside, tongued and grooved sheeting on the inside of it, and the reason I know that was that somebody broke the lock at one time, but it was not vandalised apart from that. If people were up for a walk and the rain came on it was very useful to nip in there for shelter. It was just a little wooden shed, but it was more than a shed – it was really more like a modern summerhouse. Glass windows, yes. It was square, the size of a small greenhouse. Varnished. I can't remember what it was outside, it may have been all timber outside. It wasn't brick anyway. Well, it's funny I can't remember exactly where it was, but I would say that coming out of the front door of the castle if you turned right and you took the path going up the hill, sloping up the hill, well, I imagine it was somewhere up there, in other words up to the rose gardens. Not all that near the castle, you would have thought for a child's playhouse that it would be nearer the castle than it was. Was it a child's playhouse or a summerhouse? I don't know, that's what I knew it as. It was like that.

Winnie Arbuthnot

There was a doll's house, made of wood and quite big – I could have walked inside it but it was locked. It stood up there until it fell down. It had windows on either side and a front door. A grown-up person could have gone into it. It was for the children of the Shaftesburys; it was known as the Shaftesbury children's dollhouse. It was sort of brown. Made of sheeting. I never saw the door open. It was at the back of Johnny Wallace's house, as you went up the path, level with the rose garden, on the corner by the rose garden. It was underneath the trees, not out in the open.

Antrim Road Post Office

Heather Marion Swan

I was born at 694 Antrim Road and that was the post office. My grandmother started work running the post office when she was little more than 18. She went in there as a single lady and then she married a Beamish; he was in the Royal Irish Constabulary and was from Cork. She had her two sons there, Harry and Frank. And when she retired, my father Frank took it over and I was born there in 1938. I understand that my grandmother was the first person to work in the post office – I don't know how she got the job. She was originally an Armstrong, her name was Julia. She was a very determined lady, even to the day she died she stood perfectly straight, very regal. One of her brothers was a headmaster of Randalstown School.[43]

It was a two bedroom house. When you went through the main front door you had a small hallway, then the door into the post office, which was quite a good size. You had a very broad mahogany counter and to the side you had a drop-leaf. You went in there and then into the lounge. There was a lovely stained

The Antrim Road Post Office and gate lodge in 1919 or 1920. By the door stands Julia Armstrong with her elder son Harry to her left and younger son Frank to her right. At the side of the building is part of the gate that closed across the back driveway to the castle. The rear of the building was a gate lodge which had a separate front door. Today the building is a private residence.

glass partition right up to the ceiling between the lounge and the post office. From the lounge you went into the dining room/living room and then off that by the fireplace you had stairs going up to the two bedrooms. Through a door at the back of the living room you had a larder and a kitchen and out to the yard, an outside toilet. When mummy and daddy got married they changed the larder into a small bathroom, though we still had the outside toilet and a coal hole and the big mangle and all sat out there in the yard in a lean-to. There had been just one bedroom but my father divided this to make a room for me. It was a lovely comfortable house to live in.

I understand that the Shaftesburys built the post office and connected to our house was a gate lodge for the Belfast Castle Estate where the Gillespies lived, the mother, son and daughter. It had one big lounge and a small sitting room and two bedrooms upstairs. They also had an extra bit, a downstairs bedroom; they really were very high class, they had three bedrooms! We have an old photograph of the post office and Uncle Harry wrote on the back that it was built in 1890.[44] At the gate lodge there was a gate across the drive and then they did away with it because, when the Belfast Castle was taken over for entertainment and weddings and things like that, the drive became the exit. You went in by Strathmore Park but you came out from the castle down the road beside our house so the gates then were taken away. That would have been in the 1950s or 60s. The gates were still used I would say after the Second World War. I remember the gates. They were wooden.

I think the post office would have been built for the estate and for the public as well. I would reckon that they wouldn't have had telephone lines up to the castle at that stage. Many people didn't have phones, my father delivered telegrams and then we got telegram boys who they used to send out from head office. They would have come and maybe spent a year or two years. We delivered telegrams for a long time. In the post office there was a telephone booth and you could not hear anything going on in that booth; you went in there to take the telegrams so nobody else would hear what was on the messages. And you wrote those all out by hand. Later on the messages came straight out from the post office in Royal Avenue, they would have been like ticker tape that you stuck onto the telegram. The early ones were handwritten.

People would come in and look for help. With some of them, not as literate as others, it would be, 'Frank, would you deal with that?' Mummy and daddy did a lot of work for people. When the Troubles got really bad it didn't stop people from coming to the post office but it wasn't as friendly because we had to have bullet-proof screens put up along the counter. At one stage a gun was put at our son's head, he was only two and a half at the time. You know we had a couple of raids. Daddy grabbed one fella's balaclava and the police came up with their dog. He said, 'The man went up the side of our house, up over the Cave Hill, you will get him if you go quickly.' 'Oh no, we don't use the police dogs after five o'clock.' That's the truth!

I was married out of the post office. The post office closed when daddy and mummy retired. Then the newsagents on down the road, where there is a row of shops, took it over. At that stage you had to find your premises to put your post office in. My parents gave it up around 36 years ago, that is 1974, and went to live in a private house down Parkmount Road.

Martlett Towers. Originally a large private house, it became part of the Belfast Castle Estate around the 1880s, and was used to accommodate staff. After the estate was taken over by the Corporation, it became unused and was vandalised and demolished.

Around Park Lodge, Martlett Towers and the castle stables

Winnie Arbuthnot

The terrace where I live used to be known as Martlett Row. Just up the Antrim Road from us there was a fountain that ran down there, a stream from the hill; people came for miles to drink that water, every Sunday morning. It had a metal cup on a chain, people came out of town and said their water was rotten and drank it. Then they diverted that river away, piped it underneath the road and to the golf links. A path, the Sheep's Path, went up the hill from here. We had no footpath on this side of the road, it was not put on until 1947. They measured our garden the day we moved in to take a wallop off it for that footpath but never did it until 1947 – sure my garden was twice as big.

By my house is a driveway that used to be an old entrance to Martlett Towers. When we came here labourers of the estate were living in Martlett Towers, it was put into flats. After that they all sort of moved out when war broke out – they all got better housing, and the RAF moved in. They were here for about three years during the war, a wireless unit, WSU 23 or something, and then they sent them up to Enniskillen. They took over the castle and had a couple of caravans here for wireless operating, there was one up in the walled garden and there was one at the back of Martlett Towers. The caravans were on wheels; they could attach them to a lorry and drive them away. The boys were there. We knew them, they used to come down for their supper, played darts and things. We knew them all right but I don't know what the ones in the castle did, to be truthful. They were all English, all from many parts of England.

What happened to Martlett Towers? Someone set it on fire one night. I have no idea when that was though it was long after the war. Possibly around about the 50s.[45] I wakened up one night and there was a whole furore and there were firemen in there and I just got into bed again and went to sleep! They were all a furore next morning. They said, 'Did you see it?' and I said, 'Aye, I saw the firemen', 'And did you not waken any of us?' 'No, I thought we were safe enough!' I wasn't worried, I went back to bed!

Martlett Towers was a big stone building, a massive building. It was put into four houses, they were not flats, I think they were two storey. You know, there were different doors. There was the Camerons, Mr and Mrs Cameron, and they had a son and a daughter. She later became a school teacher and taught me in school. Johnny Cameron, he was the head gardener and he was killed. There was no footpath on this side of the Antrim Road then, he got knocked down and killed. Oh, who else? The Smiths were in it. He was killed when they were felling a tree there.

There used to be wooden gates up there, on the drive to Martlett Towers, and they were closed at ten to staff in the towers. By ten o'clock they were locked out. They were wooden gates, green wooden gates. They were near the top end of Martlett Row. There had been iron gates at the bottom of the drive, down by the Antrim Road, but they disappeared during the war, they took the gates. The metal gates had always been kept open for these houses, a way into Martlett Row.

Sir Robert Baird lived in a big two storey house, Park Lodge, it became the Christian Brothers' school. He took the stone gate lodge on the driveway by my house for one of his chauffeurs, Lady Baird's chauffeur called Kirkwood. Sir Robert's chauffeur lived on the other side of the drive, in the third house in the terrace here. Baird owned the Belfast Telegraph.

There was a man Johnny Wallace – he was in charge of the grounds and he lived in a single storey house. There was a double storey house next to it that was in ruins. His house was at the back of the rose garden down on the corner. He was buried from there. A wee small man with grey hair and a moustache. He dropped dead and my mother went up to the funeral. When they brought the coffin out peacocks made a fuss. There were peacocks in the estate then.[46]

Irene Bell

If you go up the very back entrance to the castle estate, that's where there is a little stone lodge, a couple of hundred yards up the Antrim Road from the old post office. A gate lodge. Well that led to what was always known as – I always heard it called – the dower house of the castle. With the house being built on falling ground I think the stables were underneath it or something like that. The house was demolished but the flat roof of what had been the floor of the house or the roof of the stables was still there. I had always heard it called the dower house – it was always kind of known – everyone always referred to it as the dower house. We always assumed it was the dower house belonging to the Shaftesburys.[47]

Pat Kirkwood, who unfortunately died a few years ago, lived with her father in the little gate lodge at the Antrim Road. Now there were two other cottages that had been occupied by people who worked in the estate and they were round behind what was the rose garden, what's now the maze. Those two little cottages – I am not sure whether they were semi-detached, but they had definitely been occupied by workers on the estate. That would have been in the 1930s. Later I think they became completely derelict.[48]

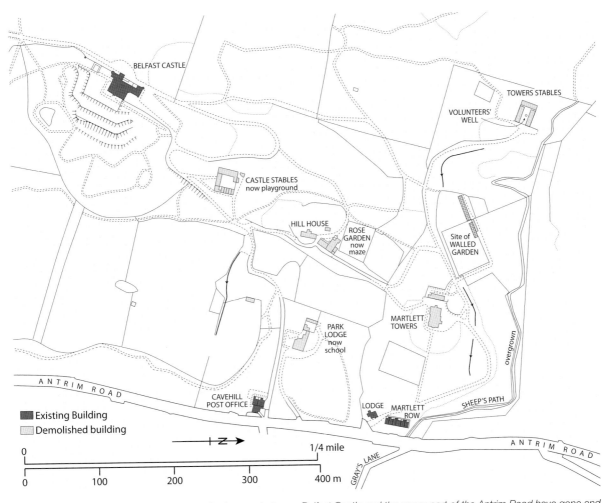

BELFAST CASTLE

TOWERS STABLES

VOLUNTEERS' WELL

CASTLE STABLES
now playground

HILL HOUSE

ROSE GARDEN
now maze

Site of WALLED GARDEN

PARK LODGE
now school

MARTLETT TOWERS

ANTRIM ROAD

CAVEHILL POST OFFICE

LODGE

MARTLETT ROW

SHEEP'S PATH

overgrown

ANTRIM ROAD

GRAY'S LANE

Existing Building
Demolished building

N

0 100 200 300 400 m

0 1/4 mile

A lost landscape. Many of the buildings in the area between Belfast Castle and the upper part of the Antrim Road have gone and only bits of walls, rubble and remnants of gardens show where they once stood. The Sheep's Path for a time marked the right of way up the hill but now that the formerly private estate grounds are open to all, the path has become overgrown and redundant.

57

Martlett Row was built in 1916 to house staff employed by the Belfast Castle Estate. It is pictured here in the 1940s, before the Antrim Road was widened. Today the houses are privately owned.

The post office on the Antrim Road – I heard it was the first purpose-built post office in Belfast, probably purpose-built for the castle. Frank Beamish was the postmaster in my day, his mother was the postmistress before that. Well, when you go up the driveway beside it there was a house. It was always known as Dobbs' house. That housed the stables for the castle. But it was quite a nice house and the back part of this house had all the stables. Today there is a playground occupying what used to be Dobbs' house. We assumed that a man called Dobbs had lived there, who looked after the horses. That house was vandalised. It was red brick as far as I can remember. A very nice house, a nice clean-looking house if you know what I mean. I can always remember the front door would look over the lough and up the side of it were great big gates and those were the gates to take the horses into the stables. A brick house, a brick wall and gates set into the brick wall. Vandals got in. The first thing was they broke into it and the next thing was the whole thing went up in flames. Because I can remember when the fire brigade came we didn't know at the time what it was, what was happening.[49]

I was past childhood, say 15, when we went up to live on the Antrim Road. A lot of us from different schools, around about five to maybe ten of us, used to go up there to climb the Cave Hill. There was no such thing as going off to town for the afternoon in those days. Usually we went up beside the post office right up past the Volunteers' Well, up as far as the Devil's Punch Bowl, round in front of the caves and to McArt's Fort that way. On our way up when we got to the top of the pine forest there used to be some kind of a wire fence or something there, there were posts and wire lying on the ground and things like that. We went over that wire which took us onto the top of the Sheep's Path. By going this route from the post office we missed the awkward lower part of the Sheep's Path which went up just behind the six little cottages on the Antrim Road, the cottages that face down Gray's Lane. Just at the far end of those cottages, that's where the Sheep's Path came onto the Antrim Road. An opening in the hedge about so wide and three concrete or maybe stone steps, steps set that way, at right angles to the hedge there. Sunk into the bank. You went up them I think sideways and then up the Sheep's Path which went up the back of the walled garden belonging to the castle and eventually to the top of Cave Hill. The walled garden when I knew it at first was still kept perfectly, entirely as a vegetable garden and fruit garden, for the castle I assume. Now that would be in the early days. But then it got worse, worse, worse, overgrown. I knew the Sheep's Path when it was the only way up there, I think probably before they opened the castle to the public. But it was known as quite a dangerous path then because it was just a rough wee path about so wide.[50]

Heather Marion Swan

Further up from the post office facing onto the Antrim Road is a row of houses that they used to call the cottages. A lot of the workers lived there. Some of them worked in the castle. Percy, the son of Sammy and Annie Armstrong, lived there. He was employed by the Corporation as a ranger, looking after the castle grounds and Bellevue. When he retired he still stayed on in the house. The Hadleys lived there, I am not too sure what they did and there was Jeanie Caldwell, I think she worked up in the castle at one stage. I think this row had been part of the estate, though at one time the Housing Executive had them.[51]

When you went up the driveway from the post office and turned round the bend there were the stables and near there was another row of houses that went years and years ago.[52] I remember the houses still standing but because there was no water or electric, people who were in there came down when any of the houses in the row on the Antrim Road became vacant. I remember Jeanie Caldwell living up there but I can't remember who else. Jeanie Caldwell, we always called her Jenny. The stables was a lovely red-bricked building and it had a big cathedral-shaped doorway, with a point. When you went in there was a cobblestoned square, with the stables off this. I don't think anybody lived there but I wouldn't like to swear to that.

Diane Hunter

I used to go up the hill past Martlett Towers quite a lot. My mother used to call it the dower house. There was a fountain in front of it somewhere. A sort of mound thing is still there by the side of the path, like a little hillock, there was a stone basin on it, but I don't think it's there anymore. The house – well, I know it was grey, but I'm not sure whether it was stone or whether it was painted. There was a building, I think it was a coach house, it was at the side of the house. It had a flat roof. Perhaps it didn't always have a flat roof. I think the top of it could have been knocked down maybe and they just left the main structure because it was sound. I walked on it, it had grass and stuff and weeds and things on it. My dog was on top of it and he just jumped off to my horror but when we scrambled down, there he was, standing there, saying 'come on, hurry up!' The dog must have landed on grass.

Near Martlett Towers there was an orchard, they looked like apple trees as far as I remember. Near this was a garden, it had brick paths and flower beds edged with brick but it wasn't looked after by the time I was in it and then I think they let it go altogether. And then there was a new effort at changing the paths. It has now been planted with rows of little trees and made into a maze. Between Martlett Towers and the stable yard there were some buildings, they were definitely standing when I was a child. I don't know if anyone was living in the house but that's the one that I think must have been a farm manager's house though my mother thought it was a curate's house but as the Chapel of the Resurrection was away over the other side of the estate, I don't think that was right. It wasn't a cottage, it was a two storey house.[53] There was what I think were pigsties so maybe it was as I said a farm manager's house or something like that. The stable yard I think was on the site where the Adventure Playground now is. I remember the stable yard standing, I don't know what they were used for at that time, perhaps they stored stuff there. There weren't any horses there then or carts or anything. It was brick and quite big, I think.

There was a big walled garden, I think it was in use, there were pot plants and things in the greenhouses but I don't know whether they bothered much with the garden bit. Later we stole one of the pots! Very big – no, not big because we had to carry it, we had to make sure no one saw us! I think we took two or three, actually. Well, the place was derelict by then you see. The glass was all broken in the greenhouses

Hill House. Winnie Arbuthnot remembers Johnny Wallace lived here and Heather Marion Swan knew this as Jeanie Caldwell's house. Diane Hunter called this the curate's house, a memory of the time when the Earl of Shaftesbury's private chaplain lived here. This photograph was taken some time after the Corporation took over the castle estate, when the buildings had become unused. Today, only rubble remains.

but there were masses of pots. If we had a car we could have taken far more! It was a very bad thing to do, but they were getting broken anyway, so. Further up the hill is the Volunteers' Well, there was a cottage somewhere near it. I think it could have been a park ranger's cottage. I remember my father talking to the man and my father must have told me that was where he lived, I suppose. Whether the ruins are still standing I don't know, it's ages since I was up there.

Alan Jones

After my apprenticeship I took on the job as propagator, responsible for growing all the bedding plants for the parks. I had that job for about four or five years. During that time because of the volume of planting, which was expanding throughout the parks, we didn't have enough space in Ormeau Nursery so we worked a number of small plots, one of which was the old walled-in garden with lean-to greenhouses at the northern end of the castle estate. That was worked for three to four years, until the Council's new nursery at Beechvale was up and running. About two years later, around 1981-2, I was fortunate enough to get the foreman's post at Belfast Castle. By that stage there had been a fire at the walled garden in the boiler house, and the glasshouses had been badly damaged and the Council had taken the decision that it wasn't worth replacing them, and the walled garden, wall and everything, was eventually demolished, unfortunately.[54] There had been just two or three lean-to glasshouses and open ground surrounded by a stone wall, one double gate and a pedestrian gate beside the glasshouses. Boiler house at the back of the wall, down below ground level. There were no pumps, it worked on the principle that hot water rises. It was coke fired. There was a guy, Joe I think his name was, and he managed it, looked after it. That was his job. That was the only building in the area, the walled-in garden.

The rose garden. When I started as foreman there was a big yew hedge that hadn't been cut, touched or maintained for probably 20-30 years, it was about 15 foot high. Inside there were no roses, just self-seeded sycamore and ash trees, 9, 10 up to 12 inches in diameter. So as one winter project we decided we would cut this yew hedge right back down and let it break away again, change it back into a formal hedge and remove all the trees growing in the garden. We started to scrape away some of the grass and moss and found brick paths and we were able to clear away enough to find the design of the rose garden. So we laid it out to exactly the same design. Now unfortunately because of the nature of the land, surrounded by fully mature trees, it wasn't ideal for roses but seeing that it was a rose garden we wanted to try to restore it back. The design wasn't complex, a circle in the middle and the paths radiated from it, like spokes of a wheel, then paths round the perimeter, a square. It had been nice to uncover the old paths and find the actual design. It's been all redone now, as a maze.

When I first came up to the castle, the road that now comes across, past the rose garden, was just a dirt track. It wasn't until I had been here about four years we got the money to put a road in, a proper Tarmac road in linking the two parts of the estate. Most people who would have come in from the back entrance, above Gray's Lane, would have just driven up the Tarmac to where the old walled garden used to be, parked the car and then would have walked on up the hill. Other people would have come up to the castle, up the main drive, parked there and would have gone back out the way they came in. So by making the new road it joined the two parts of the estate together.

THE TERRACE STEPS, BELLEVUE GARDENS, BELFAST

Bellevue

The story of Bellevue starts with the creation of gardens at Glengormley, at the terminus of the Cavehill and Whitewell Tramway, which since 1882 had operated on tracks laid along the Antrim Road. The gardens had scenic walks and a teahouse and by the late 1890s had become a place of entertainment with amusements and dancing. A key attraction was that Belfast residents could be counted as bona fide travellers after a trip up the tramlines, and could therefore legally purchase intoxicating drink on Sundays. In 1912 the Cavehill and Whitewell Tramway was acquired by Belfast Corporation and the general manager of the city transport system, Andrew Nance, identified a former tram depot just below Glengormley as a site with potential to develop new pleasure gardens. It was argued that this would provide a venue where city workers could relax in a rural setting and in addition would generate revenue for the tramways. Work soon started on developing the land, which was given the title Bellevue, a name first used for the Glengormley Gardens.[55]

The site included former quarry workings and there were costly delays caused by slippage and the new Bellevue Gardens did not open until 1920. A feature was a grand staircase decorated with flower-filled urns that led directly from the roadside tram stop up the hill to a plateau where there were band performances, open air dances and refreshments. In 1922 adjacent land at Hazelwood was purchased by the Corporation and by the early 1930s a zoo had been created and attractions at the plateau included a miniature railway. In 1936 the Floral Hall was opened on the Hazelwood site and for many years was a popular venue for dancing, complementing more formal events organised by the Tramways Committee at Belfast Castle. In 1952 there was an additional acquisition of just over nine acres of land that provided a connection between the castle estate and the pleasure grounds at Hazelwood and Bellevue to the north.[56]

In 1962, Belfast Corporation transferred the lands and activities managed by the Tramways Committee on Cave Hill to the Parks and Cemeteries Committee, which soon had to face a range of difficult decisions about Bellevue. The enclosures in the zoo were small and poorly laid out, there was a lack of interpretation and public facilities were inadequate.[57] The Bellevue Gardens, which in their heyday had been said to compare in interest and beauty to the Hanging Gardens of Babylon, suffered from vandalism and in 1970, after repeated attacks, the ornamental planters on the grand staircase were removed.[58] In addition, the Floral Hall was unable to compete with late-opening pubs and cabaret clubs. Dancing ended in 1971 and within a few years the Floral Hall was unused and redundant.[59]

In an ambitious plan, it was decided to build a new zoo that would have a strong emphasis on conservation and education. Construction started on a more spacious site adjacent to the old zoo and the first section was completed by the end of 1979. Unfortunately attempts to find a new use for the Floral Hall failed, and the grand staircase also sadly remains redundant, closed to the public and overgrown with vegetation.[60] However, a huge tract of land, stretching from the zoo through Hazelwood and the castle grounds to Carr's Glen, has been developed to form Cave Hill Country Park, Belfast's largest public space. Today access to Bellevue is via the plateau, once the site of amusements and entertainments and today a car park. From here two entrances side by side invite visitors either to the zoo or to walk footpaths laid out nearly 100 years ago by Andrew Nance that zigzag upwards through hazel trees and lead to the incomparable landscape around Cave Hill.

Winnie Arbuthnot

My mother and father went to the Floral Hall I think twice a week, great shows for three pence and six pence. The best of artists in those days. See those steps up the hill to the hall, you couldn't have moved on those steps, people going to concerts up and down. My mother and father were on them and they couldn't move backwards or forwards, such crowds came. Everyone was there and thoroughly enjoyed it. Then they closed off the steps because they were slipping, you see. Sure they let it go to wreck and ruin, they should have kept that going.

Pat Jenkins and Jim Jenkins

I started to go to the Floral Hall in 1946, when I was about 18, that was where I met my husband! There was a great big rotating silver ball reflecting the light, and the music was by Dave Glover and his orchestra, they were the regular band. There would have been hundreds of people, it was well frequented in those days. There was no alcohol, just soft drinks. They didn't serve meals. Saturday night was the main night but for a while there were other nights also. The dancing was from about half seven, eight o'clock to eleven in the evening. I don't remember the hall being used for anything else. It was fun getting up from the Antrim Road to the Floral Hall because they had a little bus called the Toast Rack which had open sides and wooden seats. And you sat on these and rattled up the long winding road from the Hazelwood gates. It would have seated about 20 people, a few minutes up then it would have come down for the next lot.

The plateau, where the big car park is now, that was a fairground. Quite a comprehensive fairground. It had a Big Dipper, Dodgems, roundabouts, shooting galleries. Mostly in the summer, quite a thing for holidaymakers because people used to – would you believe – come to Belfast for their holidays. They would have taken my sister and I to Bellevue, this would be around about 1936. It was a bustle of people. There were Pierrots singing and dancing and comedians. They were at a sort of a bandstand with seats in front. There were boats the public could hire on the pond by the Floral Hall. It was fun. Then the visitors used to win things on the coconut shy like teddy bears and give them to the children like me! There was an arcade with slot machines; it was a covered-in area. They used to have fireworks now and again in the evenings, I think towards the end of the summer. They also had a fireworks display there on VE Day and VJ Day, to celebrate the end of the war.

John Swindell

I was in the old zoo as a kid. The main attraction was more or less the steps and lots of different animals in cages. You had more contact with them in the old cages. They used to be behind bars, now they are behind glass. But back then they could throw the odd bit of muck at you! When I started working here all the land that's now the zoo was just a park, and the place where the elephants are now was a golf course, a pitch and putt, and they had little boats on a lake by the Floral Hall. When the old zoo was going they might have had 10 or 12 gardeners, they were doing flower beds. A great squad of gardeners.

It was what they called a zoological gardens. Now they don't have flower displays and the grounds are looked after by what they call flying squads, a group of grounds staff that maybe do here and park sites at Mallusk and Ballysillan.

I don't remember the Floral Hall being used for dances, when I started here it was mostly community groups using it for roller skating. Bus loads of kids. That would have been around the 1970s.[61] Unfortunately it has deteriorated through the years and now it's just used as stores – hay and stuff, crates. There were amusements on the plateau when I started here. Dodgems, go-karts, carousel and things, the usual stalls with hoops and things like that. Up here, where the zoo is now, was just really a park. What they call the Avenue, you used to be able to drive up there, along the plateau and then out by the Whitewell.

I actually started as an attendant, a sort of park ranger, here in 1978. We would have checked the toilets in the morning before the public came in, then you would have got the litter lifted out in the car park and out round the park, then sort of patrolled, kept the vandals at bay. Then the head keeper, Bob Thompson, asked me if I was interested in being a keeper. I told him yes and then I got the interview for that. Then they started building things up here, I think the spider monkeys were one of the first and the house for the sitatungas, they are swamp deer, like an antelope. People from Enterprise Ulster did it, they built most of the enclosures.

I remember Tina getting shifted from the old elephant house. There was a moat round Tina's paddock in the old zoo and they got contractors in to build a bridge across it and they put chains round her legs and tried to pull her legs using the tractor to make her walk but she wouldn't have any of it. So, what we did was, there used to be a man here, Dennis Quinn, who had been here since a boy, and he was a bit childish if you know what I mean, he had childish ways, and Tina loved him. That's how I got Tina into the container to bring her up to the new zoo. I gave Dennis the bag of food and Dennis walked into the container and Tina followed him. No chains round her legs. Just him and me, I asked him to go into the container with the bag of food and she followed and I put the scaffolding bars across so she couldn't get out again. Then we took the container up the Antrim Road and into the new elephant house. That was exciting that day. Tina is still here, she has been at Belfast zoo since she was a baby. Brought in here I think in 1965 or 1966, one of the characters of the zoo, she used to take handbags and things like that and searched them. Only a few people could have worked with her because she played other people up. She was mischievous if you know what I mean, hit them a wee pat with the trunk and then they would have bolted outside, backed off from her. If you just told her to behave she was alright but if you let her off with it she would have just kept you going more, you know. I worked with the elephants for about 20 years but it's all changed. Now there is not much contact with the animals. I would have walked into the elephant house but now with all this health and safety there are procedures in all zoos.

Craig Wallace

I remember as a small child going with my sister and parents to see animals in the menagerie, a small menagerie that was on the plateau, where the zoo car park is now. From memory it seemed to have been a circle of cages, 15 or 25 cages each with an animal, mostly the big cats. You walked around the circle, and that was that. Then the Corporation decided that they would have a new zoo at Bellevue, which was out of date by the time that it was opened in 1934. It was really a postage stamp collection. You had one lion, one tiger, one leopard, one elephant. The main cages were placed at the side of the plateau, backing onto the escarpment and faced east. They never got the sun. We were captivated as children, of course, but when you think back on it now, it was pretty awful.

Bellevue was well known for its gardens, there was this huge rock garden with limestone rocks. The grand staircase up from the Antrim Road was also known as the floral staircase, they had hanging baskets and so on, containers on both sides of the staircase. There was a rockery at the top of the stairs on the right. I met the head gardener many, many years ago, long after he had retired and I was shown an old plan of the rock garden. The standard of horticulture in the old zoo was high. They took great pride in the floral decoration. And as far as I remember there were hanging baskets in the monkey house! You could walk inside the monkey house, with enclosures on both sides, and in my recollection there were hanging baskets in that area.

There was a teahouse that was part of the original farmhouse and I remember going out to Greenisland and met a lady who had lived in that house as a child. This teahouse later got into disrepair. I remember going up with a colleague one day for tea, just to see the place, and it was pretty awful. Very poor management. We decided that we would have to do something about it and I remember picking new crockery, it was part of my job, having an array of crockery in front of me to see which one we should pick! Shortly after that it was destroyed during the Troubles, burnt.

Then the idea of a new zoo came around. And I remember walking with the chairman of the Parks Committee and colleagues around the Hazelwood site. There was a pitch and putt course there and the Floral Hall and there had been boats on the lake. The Floral Hall really stopped being used in the mid-1960s. That kind of socialising had ceased to be popular, the 'Palais de Dance'. It had ceased functioning when I became director of parks in 1972, it was a storehouse for the zoo though the pitch and putt course was quite popular.

There were also still amusements on the plateau. It was completely separate from the zoo and Floral Hall, they must have paid a yearly rent to the Council. There were bumper cars, swings, the usual. As far as I recall there was a Miss Barry who lived there on-site in a caravan but it was managed by two brothers, the Wallace brothers. They appeared to be the proprietors of the amusement park. But when the new zoo was created at the Hazelwood site in the late 1970s, obviously we required the plateau area to provide as much car parking space as possible. And I didn't like the juxtaposition of an amusement park and a zoo, because very often the amusements attracted rowdies. There was opposition even from within the Council to removing the amusements, but I managed with my then committee chairman's help to get it closed.[62]

Old zoo entrance in the 1970s.

Several of the staff went to visit zoos in England and Europe and they came back with a report in about 1974 and then zoo consultants were appointed and they planned the new zoo. The first enclosure in the zoo was opened I think in 1978 and I think we had a parks luncheon to commemorate this. It is on a very steep slope, that's the great problem. For elderly people the steep slope would not be conducive to walk right up to the top. The idea behind it right from the beginning was the breeding of rare species, Asiatic lions rather than African lions and many of the colobus monkeys, tiny monkeys that are under threat in the wild. They were very successful in the breeding program, right from the beginning. There were Irish rare breeds kept at the zoo also. In more recent years there has been more publicity about the zoo, I think the publicity has been excellent. I used to keep a census of the visitors and the lowest I had was 66,000 and when I left it had gone up to 250,000 and I gather that it goes beyond that today.

You know there used to be a tradition of people going up Cave Hill at Easter time, up on the slopes where there would be games and drinking. The population of Belfast went out to enjoy themselves. Well, that tradition does continue to the present day, by people going up to the zoo at Easter. I have never seen anything like it, at Easter there isn't room for the cars, people have to park on the Antrim Road. Easter is a big time in Belfast.

Notes and References

(In the following notes the abbreviation PRONI is used for the Public Record Office of Northern Ireland. The Belfast Parks correspondence files referred to are currently (2010) stored in the basement of Malone House and can only be viewed by permission of Belfast City Council.)

1. It is likely that for hundreds of years people have pointed out the profile of a face on Cave Hill and by the early 19th century the association with Napoleon was well established, for example in 1830 it was noted that '...the citizens of Belfast take pleasure in directing the attention of strangers to a curious resemblance which has been discovered between the outline of the mountain, and the profile of the unfortunate Napoleon'. William Millar, *Ten views of picturesque scenery in the north and northeast of Ireland* (Dublin: W. Curry & Co., 1830). The top of Cave Hill was also seen as representing the cap of liberty, for example, see Francis Joseph Bigger, 'Sports on Cave Hill. The Easter Holiday', *Belfast Telegraph*, 31 March 1923, p. 6. The suggestion that Swift might have been inspired by Cave Hill has gained popularity with plans to create public open space on the North Foreshore to be called 'The Giant's Park', though this appears to be a recent story.

2. Most authors have suggested that the caves were probably part natural but modified by man. See for example George Benn, *The History of the Town of Belfast* (Belfast: A. Mackay Junr., 1823), p. 235; A. A. Dickson, 'The cavalcade of Cave Hill', Belfast Telegraph, 12 August 1939, p. 8. The only survey that has been undertaken of the caves concluded that they were man-made. See Philip Reynolds and Samuel Turner, 'The caves in Ben Madighan', *Ulster Journal of Archaeology*, 8. (1902), pp. 73-82.

3. Rev. James O'Laverty, *An historical account of the diocese of Down and Connor*, Vol. 2, (Dublin: M.H. Gill & Son, 1880), p. 455.

4. Rev. W. M. O'Hanlon, *Walks among the poor of Belfast and suggestions for their improvement* (Belfast: Mayne, Printer, 1853), pp. 34-35.

5. The story of the Cave Hill diamond gained prominence when, in the 1880s, a stone described as 'a very good example of the Irish diamond' was found by a boy on Cave Hill. This was acquired by John Erskine, who displayed it in his hat shop in North Street. Erskine was an enthusiastic publicist, the Belfast Naturalists' Field Club excursion to Cave Hill in 1890 noted '...a mysterious, but by no means ornamental inscription, high up on the rocks, ...a eulogistic reference to the goods of a certain enterprising hatter in North Street'. For details, see George Henry Bassett, *County Antrim 100 years ago: a guide and directory 1888* (Belfast: Friar's Bush Press, 1989), p. 201; Anon, 'Cave Hill', *Annual report and proceedings of the Belfast Naturalists' Field Club*, 2:3. (1890), pp. 272-275; Anon, 'Random notes and notions', *Ulster Saturday Night*, 23 February 1895, p. 1; W. N. C. Barr, *Derriaghy: A short history of the Parish revised, added to and updated* (Dunmurry: The Very Reverent W. N. C. Barr, 2006), p. 165; Anon, *The Cave Hill Diamond* (Belfast: Linen Hill Library, 2009).

6. Cathal O'Byrne, *As I roved out: A book of the North* (Belfast: The Irish News Ltd., 1946), pp. 248-252. Rocks referred to as seats or thrones are quite common in Ireland. O'Laverty noted an example on the top of Slemish in County Antrim, '...a place called the "Priest's Chair", it is a natural cleft in the rock which has produced the accidental form of a seat'. See Rev. James O'Laverty, *An historical account of the diocese of Down and Connor*, Vol. 3 (Dublin: M.H. Gill & Son, 1881), pp. 437-438. W. G. Wood-Martin, *Traces of the elder faiths of Ireland*, Vol. 2 (London: Longmans, Green, and Co., 1902), pp. 251-256, provides a number of other examples.

7. George Benn, *The History of the Town of Belfast* (Belfast: A. Mackay Junr., 1823), p. 209; John Gray, 'The sports of Easter Monday', Irish Pages, 5:1. (2009), pp. 197-211.

   The tradition of egg rolling was described in the Ordnance Survey Memoirs of 1838-9: 'On Easter Monday and Tuesday the young and old of both sexes from the surrounding districts, but particularly from Belfast, congregate on the summit of the Cave Hill...and there spend these days in a variety of amusements, of which rolling painted or dyed eggs is the most characteristic or favourite. Tents are pitched and spirits and refreshments in great variety are exposed for sale. This is a season anxiously looked forward to by the younger members of the families.' See A. Day and P. McWilliams, *Ordnance Survey Memoirs of Ireland: Parishes of County Antrim 1, 1838-9*, Vol. 2 (Belfast: Institute of Irish Studies, Queen's University, 1990), pp. 112-3. An earlier reference of 1819 specifically refers to women and children gathering and trundling hard-boiled, dyed eggs down slopes at Easter in the Belfast area and interestingly states that egg rolling was practiced only by Presbyterians, which if correct, might suggest that this was a tradition introduced from Scotland. See William Shaw Mason, *A Statistical Account or Parochial Survey of Ireland*, Vol. 3 (Dublin: Faulkner-Press, 1819), pp. 207-208.

8. William Theobald Wolfe Tone, *Life of Theobald Wolfe Tone* (Dublin: The Lilliput Press, 1998), pp. 107-108.

9. Anon, 'Belfast', *Belfast News-Letter*, 4 June - 7 June 1782, p. 2.

10. John Gray, *The Great Cave Hill Right of Way Case* (Belfast: Cave Hill Conservation Campaign, 2010).

11. For examples of academic pursuits on the hill, see Anon, 'Geological excursion to Cave Hill', *Belfast News-Letter*, 15 April 1881, p. 2; Anon, 'Ben Madighan or the Cavehill and the Belfast Art Society', *The Northern Whig*, 22 July 1891, p. 6; accounts of several excursions to Cave Hill in issues of the *Annual report and proceedings of the Belfast Naturalists' Field Club*.

12. Today the main areas on Cave Hill for egg rolling are the steep mown banks at the seaward side of the castle garden and the steep mown slope by the main drive by the car park just before the castle. The only other place around Belfast known to the author where people still congregate in numbers to roll eggs is the Giant's Ring near Edenderry.

13. Stewart McFetridge, *The Cavehill waggon line: Belfast's forgotten railway*, (Newtownabbey: The White House, 1999); Colin J. Robb, 'Carr's Glen – link with a forgotten family', *Belfast Telegraph*, 10 July 1954, p. 4.

14. Robert Scott, *A Breath of Fresh Air: The Story of Belfast's Parks* (Belfast: Blackstaff Press, 2000), p. 150.

15. The McConnell and Craig families are first listed in the *Belfast Street Directory* in 1909 (in the entries for Ballysillan Road) with Samuel McConnell, farmer and dairyman, at Glencar and Robert Craig, labourer, in Upper Carr's Glen. Samuel McConnell was followed at Glencar by Joseph McConnell, who was last listed in 1959. An entry under Carr's Glen in 1965 for Violet Craig was the final reference to this family in Carr's Glen. Prior to 1909 there is a reference in the directory to J. Kirk, beetler, who perhaps was employed at the beetling mill in Carr's Glen prior to it becoming redundant and used as a residence by the Craigs.

16. Alan Boyd, 'A short history of the Belfast and Cavehill Railway Company', *North Belfast Historical Magazine, 2* (1986), pp. 5-8; Stewart McFetridge, *The Cavehill waggon line: Belfast's forgotten railway* (Newtownabbey: The White House, 1999).

17. Belfast Parks correspondence files; Conveyance of lands at Cavehill: Northern Bank Executor and Trustee Company Limited to Belfast City Council, 23 January 1989. Copy held by Belfast City Council.

18. Cave Hill is the ideal place for beacons that would be visible throughout the region. 'On the evening of the Prince of Wales's wedding-day, in 1863, one hundred tar barrels were carried on to the top of the Cave Hill and lighted, and on the evening of Queen Victoria's jubilee in 1887 there were similar illuminations.' See H. Mayne Knox, 'History of the Cave Hill', *The Northern Whig*, 9 March 1911, p. 6.

19. Sam Moore has privately circulated his memories in a booklet entitled *Daddystown*, produced December 2007.

20. See The Roamer, 'Norah's grave still causes tears to fall' *News-Letter*, 1 December 1988, p. 13; Anon, 'Romantic murder and suicide in Belfast', *Belfast Evening Star*, 12 March 1890, p. 3; Anon, 'The terrible tragedy at Cave Hill', *Belfast Evening Star*, 13 March 1890, p. 3.

The wall referred to by Mr Jenkins, which can be traced going up the hill towards the quarry where it turns and runs along the slope of the hill towards McArt's Fort, was originally the southern and western boundaries of a deer park on Cave Hill and subsequently formed part of the boundary of the Belfast Castle Estate. Today only a few short sections of this wall of rough blocks of stone still stand to its original height (c. 2m high and c. 50cm thick). It is known that there were deer on Cave Hill until 1859 and the 'black palings' recalled by Mr Jenkins may have been deer fencing constructed along the boundary of the estate where the original wall had collapsed. See Ben Simon, *If trees could talk: The story of woodlands around Belfast* (Belfast: The Forest of Belfast, 2009).

21. Ben Simon, *If trees could talk: The story of woodlands around Belfast* (Belfast: The Forest of Belfast, 2009), pp. 21, 30-33, 64-65.

22. Anon, 'Hints representing the improvement of Belfast', *Belfast News-Letter*, 16-19 February 1790, p. 3.

23. See Ben Simon, *If trees could talk: The story of woodlands around Belfast* (Belfast: The Forest of Belfast, 2009), pp. 64-65; Anon, 'Consecration of the mortuary chapel on Lord Donegall's demesne lands', *Belfast News-Letter*, 21 December 1869, p. 3; The building of the lodge and 'stable offices' are referred to in letters from James Torrens to John Lanyon dated 31 August 1870 and from W. H Lynn to the Marquis of Donegall dated 8 February 1878. See PRONI D/811/399/1.

24. The original documents for the acquisition of land to the north of the deer park have not been located, though some details are given in: Agreement between The Right Honourable The Earl of Shaftesbury and Lord Ashley with the Lord Mayor, Aldermen, and citizens of the City of Belfast, dated 21 March 1935; Conveyance between The Right Honourable the Earl of Shaftesbury the Honourable Antony

Ashley the Honourable Hugo Baring the Belfast Corporation, dated 3 May 1935. Copies held by Belfast City Council.

The date of construction of the small estate buildings has not been determined, though the post office is known to have opened in 1893 (see reference 44), Martlett Tower Cottages are first mentioned in the *Belfast Street Directory* of 1916 and the style of architecture of the gamekeeper's cottage suggests that it dates from around the same period as the post office. Park Lodge, a large building by the Antrim Road, was also purchased by the castle estate, probably as part of the acquisition of Martlett Towers. However, as Park Lodge was always leased and never functioned as part of the castle estate, it has been excluded from this account of the estate lands.

25. Anon, 'Death of the Marquis of Donegall K. P.,' *Belfast News-Letter*, 22 October 1883, p. 5.

26. An article of 1892 referred to the castle as being occupied by the Countess of Shaftesbury '...for several months in the year'. Following her death in 1898, her son, the 9th Earl of Shaftesbury, was resident for several years and was mayor of Belfast in 1907. However, by 1921, a newspaper report suggested that Belfast Castle might be leased and referred to '...increasing indications of the severance of his Lordship's more intimate personal ties with the city...'. See John Vinycomb, 'Historical and descriptive account of the city of Belfast', *Journal of the Royal Society of Antiquaries of Ireland, 22* (1892), pp. 323-333; Anon, 'Sir T. Dixon leases Belfast Castle', *Belfast Telegraph*, 7 September 1921, p. 6.

27. Anon, 'Shaftesbury Estate', *Belfast Telegraph*, 13 November 1933, p. 10; Anon, 'Belfast Castle presented to the city', *Belfast Telegraph*, 27 January 1934, p. 5.

28. A letter to a newspaper in 1937 criticised proposals to develop a golf course in the castle grounds as being '...enough to make the angels weep'. In a subsequent newspaper article summarising the decision to raise a loan to develop the castle estate, one Alderman criticised the scheme, calling the Tramways Committee '...a full-blown hobby-horse committee' and added that '...he understood that it was proposed to besmear the beautiful hillside of the castle with anything from a slot machine up'. See 'Letter to the Editor', *Northern Whig and Belfast Post*, 23 January 1937, p. 11; Anon, 'Belfast Castle: Development plan passed', *Northern Whig and Belfast Post*, 2 February 1937, p. 3.

29. A report of 1969 produced for Belfast City Council quotes earlier Belfast Corporation files and states that '...the Castle was requisitioned by Crown forces during the war and was occupied by the R.A.F. from 7th September, 1940 to 31st October, 1941 and transferred to the Admiralty on 1st November, 1941 when it became the H.Q. of Flag Officer commanding Northern Ireland. The Castle was released from requisition on 1st April, 1946 and later that month the Ministry of Finance authorised the spending of £1,800 by the Corporation on restoration and redecoration'. See P. Coyle, 'A report Belfast Castle Structure, Condition and Use', September 1969. Copy in Belfast Parks correspondence files.

The minutes of the Belfast Corporation Transport Committee meetings of 9 October 1940, 11 September 1940 and 13 August 1941 state that Martlett Towers, Belfast Castle, stables and yard and also Caldwell's house and Wallace's house were requisitioned. The latter two premises are thought to be the buildings elsewhere called Hill House that were located by the rose garden. See PRONI LA/7/26AA/13.

30. See Anon, 'Plan for castle as hotel refused', *Belfast Telegraph*, 8 December 1971, p. 14; Anon, 'Castle cannot become hotel, says ministry', *News Letter*, 31 December 1971, p. 7.

31. Anon, 'All this could one day be yours', *Sunday News*, 1 December 1974, p. 15.

32. Denis Haslam, *Belfast Castle condition report*, Anthony F. Lucy and Company, Chartered Architects, 13 Lombard Street, Belfast, June 1978. Copy in Belfast Parks correspondence files.

33. The main floors reopened in 1988 and the basement was subsequently developed. See Anon, 'Belfast Castle', *Ulster Architect*, September 1987, pp. 4-10; Ken Devlin, 'Castle gets a facelift', *Belfast Telegraph*, 7 September 1988, p. 3; Anon, 'Belfast Castle's basement', *Ulster Architect*, July/August 1990, pp. 14-16.

34. Anon, 'Green "lungs" will help city of future', *News Letter*, 11 October 1989, p. 15; Anon, *Cave Hill Country Park Development Plan*, Belfast City Council Parks Department, November 1990. Copy in Belfast Parks correspondence files.

35. Only a few brief references to the role Belfast played as a naval base and activities at Belfast Castle have been published. See John W. Blake, *Northern Ireland in the Second World War*, (Belfast: Her Majesty's Stationery Office, 1956) pp. 333-334; R. S. Allison, *HMS Caroline* (Belfast: Blackstaff Press, 1973) pp. 117-20; Christian Lamb, *I Only Joined for the Hat: Redoubtable Wrens at War – Their Trials, Tribulations and Triumphs* (London: Bene Factum Publishing Ltd., 2007). The website www.liverpoolwarmuseum.co.uk (accessed 01/08/10) gives some information about the Western Approaches Command, which from 1941 was based at Derby House, Liverpool.

36. The Belfast Corporation minute books contain a wealth of incidental details, including a note that natural history specimens donated by Colonel G. Pennefather Evans CBE in 1947 were on display at the castle. Belfast Corporation Transport Committee minutes, 22 January 1947, p. 286. PRONI LA7/26AA/14.

37. Craig's memory was quite correct. Hastings had a catering concession for all of the food outlets run by Belfast Parks for five years from 1966 to 1971. The outlets were Malone House, Belfast Castle, Floral Hall, the bungalow cafe at Hazelwood and the zoo restaurant and kiosk. Information from Belfast Parks correspondence files.

38. The fire, which was started maliciously and badly damaged the ballroom of the castle, was on the night of 30 October 1982. A window had been broken and inflammable liquid poured in and set alight. In response to this incident, security fencing was installed around the boundary of the castle and gardens. See Belfast Parks correspondence files; David Simpson, '"Cage" around a castle gets ratepayers rattled', *Belfast Telegraph*, 21 January 1983.

39. A number of former Belfast Parks staff have been asked about the cannons and Belfast Parks files have been searched for information and parts of what appears to be quite a complicated story can be unravelled.

The oldest reference in the Belfast Parks correspondence files found regarding the discovery of cannons refers not to Ormeau but to Belfast Castle. In February 1964, the director of parks wrote identical short letters to W. A. Seaby, director of the Ulster Museum, and to G. Thompson, curator of the Folk Museum, to state that five cannons that had been found in the rubbish heap at Belfast Castle and that 'before disposing of them as scrap' he asked if the cannons might be of interest to them. Mr Thompson replied to say that they would not be suitable for the Folk Museum, though Mr Seaby asked to see the cannons and on 28/02/64 wrote to the director of parks to acknowledge receipt of a gift of 'Two cannons, 17th century. Eight gun-carriage wheels.'

Robert Scott (parks conservation and education manager) has noticed that photographs of Belfast Castle from the Lawrence Collection dating from around 1900 show cannons on carriages in the castle garden and, by comparing different views, at least five or perhaps six cannons can be identified. It seems certain that these were the cannons that were at some later date thrown on the dump at the castle and found in 1964.

Craig Wallace was asked about the discovery of cannons at Belfast Castle but this had predated his involvement in Parks. However, he recalled cannon(s) being found at the nearby Belfast zoo. John Stronge, former zoo manager, confirmed that around 1971 there had been several cannons, he thinks three, lying at the side of the plateau (now the car park), though he did not know what had happened to them. The subsequent find of cannon(s) at Ormeau mentioned by Alan Jones has independently been confirmed to the author by Alan Wilson and Reg Maxwell (former parks area managers), though no one was certain how many cannon(s) were found in Ormea Yard.

The simplest explanation for these finds is that after the Ulster Museum were given two of the cannons found at the castle, the remaining three were not disposed of for scrap but were moved to the zoo and subsequently to Ormeau. However, it is possible that these were separate discoveries of cannon(s).

A letter has been located in Belfast Parks correspondence files from T. J. Wylie of Ulster Museum to Craig Wallace dated 10/02/81 providing advice on the construction of carriages and Craig has a clear memory of putting in an order to Council joiners to make carriages for cannon(s). Another letter from Wylie to Craig dated 06/05/81 discussed the possibility of the parks having on long term loan the two cannons acquired by the museum, though it is not known if this happened. Both Craig and Robert Scott recall that once carriages were made cannons were temporarily moved to Fernhill House (then parks headquarters) before being moved to Belfast Castle. Today there are three cannons on carriages at the main entrance to Belfast Castle.

Finally, it is interesting to speculate where the cannons came from prior to being used as ornaments in the garden of Belfast Castle. One of the three cannons currently at the entrance to the mansion has in raised letters the inscription 'MARQs DONEGALL', indicating that it was long the property of the family. It seems likely that the cannons had been at the house built by the Donegalls in the early 19th century at Ormeau, perhaps at the site by the Lagan marked 'battery' on the first edition six inch Ordnance Survey map, and were moved to Cave Hill when the third Marquis built Belfast Castle.

40. Mr Armstrong, gamekeeper, is first mentioned in the Belfast Street Directory in 1923, though he was employed in the castle estate in the previous year, when he made the gruesome discovery of the body of a child who had been murdered in the woods. See Anon, 'Belfast child's tragic fate. Murder on Cave Hill', *Weekly Telegraph*, 10 June 1922, p. 5; Anon, 'The Cavehill murder. Man charged with crime', *Weekly Telegraph*, 17 June 1922 p. 2; Anon, 'Cavehill atrocity', *Weekly Telegraph*, 8 July 1922, p. 5.

After the estate was taken over by the Corporation some employees including Samuel Armstrong were permitted to remain, see Transport Committee minutes of 15 February 1950, p. 256. The Armstrongs appear to have left around 1950, when the Transport Committee minutes of 26 April 1950 noted that the gamekeeper's house was to be let to the head keeper at the zoo. The building was subsequently rented to the Scouts. PRONI LA/26AA/15.

41. Harry Porter kindly located Scout records that include a docket for three keys to the gamekeeper's cottage received from the Corporation Transport Department on 27 July 1954 and a letter from the Scouts to the Corporation to inform them that the cottage had been destroyed by fire around 9.30pm on 20 March 1957. Harry also kindly located a short newspaper article about the fire (*Belfast News-Letter*, 21 March 1957, p. 4), which referred to the building as a single storey brick-built Scout hall and noted that the fire brigade had tried to put out the fire by pumping water all the way from Strathmore Park. The minutes of the Belfast Corporation Transport Committee meeting of 3 April 1957 also noted that the building had been destroyed on 20 March 1957. PRONI LA/7/26AA/17.

42. The *Belfast Street Directory* mentions James Greer as a gamekeeper at the Belfast Castle Estate from 1915 to 1921. In the early part of the 20th century the directory lists two gamekeepers at the castle, though after Mr Greer left, only one gamekeeper, Mr Armstrong, was employed. The work of the gamekeeper and the risks associated with the profession can be seen from reports from 1875 when a gamekeeper called James Houston died after being shot by a poacher in the castle grounds. See Anon, 'The late case of shooting at the Cave Hill', *Belfast News-Letter*, 29 October 1875, p. 3 and subsequent issues of the paper which covered the inquest.

43. Julia Armstrong is named as an early postmistress, though she was not the first. The *Belfast Street Directory* gives Margaret Craig as postmistress from 1893 to 1894, Mary Sampson from 1895 to 1897 and Julia Armstrong (Beamish) from 1898 to 1940.

44. Kevin McShane of the North of Ireland Philatelic Society kindly provided information about the Cave Hill Post Office from the Tony Graham Archive held by the Society. This included a reference from Irish Post Office records (PRONI MIC 522/B) concerning the Earl of Shaftesbury who signed a deed dated 14 June 1892 to act as guarantee for the proposed office at Cave Hill, as it was considered to be potentially uneconomic. As suggested by Heather Marion Swan, his interest in the venture was probably because it would improve communications for Belfast Castle.

Kevin McShane also kindly informed the author that the Cave Hill Post Office opened on 21 June 1893, the event anticipated by a note on page 4 of the *Belfast News-Letter* of this date. 'New Postal and Telegraph Office – A postal and telegraph office will be opened today (Wednesday) at Cave Hill, at one of the entrances to Belfast Castle, for the collection and delivery of telegrams, sale of stamps, and registration of letters and parcels. Hours of attendance - 7am till 8pm.'

45. In June 1957, the Transport Committee of Belfast Corporation had decided to demolish Martlett Towers, but before this could happen the building was burnt by vandals on 17 July 1957, completely destroying the interior and leaving just the walls standing. The remains were subsequently demolished. See Transport Committee Minutes 7 August 1957 p. 191. PRONI LA/7/26AA/17.

46. The history of Sir Robert Baird's house, Park Lodge, is described in Anon, 'Tower and its effigy', *Belfast Telegraph*, 31 January 1934, p. 10.

The names and professions of staff who lived in the castle estate including the people described by Winnie Arbuthnot are noted in the *Belfast Street Directory*. For example, Wallace and Cameron both first appear in the directory in 1901 and are described as gardeners. Wallace soon became land steward and is last listed in 1930, after which Cameron became land steward. Records for the castle estate also contain some fascinating details about the staff. For example, in the *Earl of Shaftesbury letter-book* (PRONI D/1080/1/4 pp. 834-835), a letter of 31 January 1934, written to the Earl of Shaftesbury at a time when the transfer of the castle estate to the Belfast Corporation was being considered, includes the following comments:

About the people living on the place, there are none in receipt of regular pensions. Mrs. Wallace and Mrs. Cameron have each a free house and coal but no money allowance. Mrs. Wallace is not badly off as her husband managed somehow or other to save a considerable sum. Mrs. Cameron has, I think, nothing of her own but her daughter, May, is earning a very good salary as a school teacher. The son, I am afraid, is still out of work.

As regards the others, old Smith has not been receiving any wages for some time as he had been past work but he lives with his son at Martlett Towers. Caldwell has been a long time in your service and I am afraid it would be very difficult for him to find employment. He lives now at the Hill in the house beside Mrs. Wallace. The other man Hoy is comparatively young. He is married and has a family.

As to Armstrong, I don't know whether he is likely to find employment elsewhere but I see no reason why he should not do so, and as to Kane I think there ought to be no difficulty in getting a job for him as he is a very reliable man and capable.

I am afraid Gillespie is past doing anything but the very lightest of work. Pennell should be able to do something if he can get a job.

47. This building was Martlett Towers. Traditionally, the wife of the owner of an estate would often vacate the mansion house on the death of her husband and move to a smaller house in the grounds known as

the dower house, thereby allowing the new heir to occupy the mansion house. Although it is easy to see how Martlett Towers might be thought of as having been a dower house, as it was a substantial dwelling in the grounds of Belfast Castle, no information has been found to suggest that it was ever lived in by any member of the Donegall or Shaftesbury families. It had been built as a separate property, the residence of Joseph Magill, and when this house and its grounds became part of the Belfast Castle Estate it was converted into accommodation for estate workers. See Francis Joseph Bigger, 'Cavehill and its story. Famous right of way trial', *Belfast Telegraph*, 17 April 1925.

48. The two cottages Irene Bell recalled that were by the rose garden (now the maze) are the houses mentioned by Winnie Arbuthnot as having been Johnny Wallace's residence. This little group of buildings is referred to in the *Belfast Street Directory* as Hill House. The minutes of Belfast Corporation Transport Committee of 28 June 1938, p. 233 and 7 September 1938, p. 255 refer to 'two cottages known as The Hill' which it was proposed they demolish, though it appears that they were left to decay and collapse. See PRONI LA7/26AA/12.

Hill House and its outbuildings are shown on the first edition six-inch Ordnance Survey map of 1832-33 and therefore predate the construction of both Belfast Castle and Martlett Towers. Details of land ownership in the area during the early 19th century given in the report of a right of way trial and also in an article by Francis Bigger indicate that, prior to the acquisition of this land by the castle estate, these buildings had been occupied by Mr Orr, who was described as the 'landlord from the top of Cave Hill to the Whitehouse Road' and subsequently by Mr Nash, who is said to have enlarged Orr's house and added a second storey. See Anon, 'Report of the trial of the indictment the Queen v. Magill, tried at the County of Antrim summer assizes, 1859, before the Lord Chief Baron Pigot', *The Northern Whig*, 1859, pp. 4, 5, 13, 23; Francis Bigger, 'Cavehill and its story. Famous right of way trial', *Belfast Telegraph*, 17 April 1925. See also map of the estate PRONI D/971 M 3.

49. John Dobbs, described as 'a man who deals in high class horses', rented the stable yard buildings and a field from Lord Shaftesbury in 1933 for £70/year, an agreement that continued after Belfast Corporation acquired Belfast Castle and grounds until 1936. See *Earl of Shaftesbury letter-book*, pp. 593, 730. PRONI D/1080/1/4; Agreement between The Right Honourable The Earl of Shaftesbury and Lord Ashley with The Lord Mayor, Alderman and citizens of the city of Belfast, dated 21 March 1935, copy held by Belfast City Council; Minutes of the Tramways sub-committee meeting, 25 March 1936, p. 879. PRONI LA/7/26AA/11.

A letter of 3 October 1963 from the catering and entertainments manager to the director of parks reported that '...at approximately 5.40pm last evening, when proceeding to Belfast Castle via the back road, I noticed, when passing the old stables, that there was a fire inside the building'. A letter of 7 October 1964 to the Commissioners of Valuation from the director of parks stated that it was intended to demolish the remains of the stables (referred to as 'Dobb's Yard') and requested a reduction in the valuation. For details see Belfast Parks correspondence files.

50. The history of the Sheep's Path is given by John Gray, *The Great Cave Hill Right of Way Case* (Belfast: Cave Hill Conservation Campaign, 2010). At different times the path had different routes and Irene Bell describes both a path through the castle estate by the Volunteers' Well and a steep path by the northern boundary of the estate that started by Martlett Row.

51. These houses are Martlett Cottages, also known as Martlett Row.

52. This was the group of buildings known as Hill House. See reference 48.

53. This is Hill House. The reference to the curate is a fascinating memory. Lord Shaftesbury had a private chaplain, the Rev. Richard Brome de Bary, who officiated services at the Chapel of the Resurrection and at the oratory built in the basement of Belfast Castle and is described as having lived in a cottage in the demesne. See Richard S. Breene, *The Golden Jubilee Book of St. Peter's Church, Belfast* (Belfast: H. R. Carter Publications, 1950), p. 73. The *Belfast Street Directory* records Rev. Richard Brome de Bary as living at Hill House from 1909 to 1916. See also reference 48 for the history of this residence.

54. Belfast Parks correspondence files describe the destruction of the walled garden. On 25 February 1974, the top of the wall was broken down, a grass cutting machine was burnt and 40 panes of glass broken. On 27 February 1974, 125 panes of glass broken. On 28 February 1974, 70 panes broken.

55. Stewart McFetridge, *Bellevue: Belfast's mountain playground. Things you didn't know or had forgotten* (Belfast: The White House, 1996).

56. Mrs Barbara Noel Adeley to Belfast Corporation Conveyance dated 23 October 1952. Copy held by Belfast City Council.

57. An article about the old zoo published in 1978 noted 'A visit to the Belfast Zoo could be the experience of a lifetime, but not one you might want to repeat'. Alf McCreary, 'The not so human zoo', *Belfast Telegraph*, 1 June 1978, p. 12.

58. Anon, *The Belfast Book. 1929. Local Government in the City and County Borough of Belfast* (Belfast: R. Carswell and Son Ltd., 1929), pp. 171-173; Belfast Parks correspondence files for the zoo.

59. Belfast Parks correspondence files indicate that the key issue in deciding to close the Floral Hall was competition from late opening pubs and licensed cabaret clubs. See also Colin McClelland, 'Bloom is off the Floral Hall', *News Letter*, 31 August 1971, p. 4.

60. The completion of the first stage of the new zoo was announced in the *News Letter*, 12 December 1979, p. 2. A proposal to develop a new botanical and zoological interpretative and research centre at the Floral Hall in partnership with the Ulster Museum unfortunately did not attract the necessary funding and subsequent plans have been unsuccessful. See Laurence White, 'Plans to put Belfast zoo on world map', *Belfast Telegraph*, 4 January 1980, p. 9.

61. Roller skating at the Floral Hall was introduced in the mid-1960s and proved popular, continuing for a number of years after dances had stopped.

62. Pauline Berry's amusements at the plateau are described by Stewart McFetridge, *Bellevue: Belfast's Mountain Playground. Things you didn't know or had forgotten* (Belfast: The White House, 1996), pp. 89-90; James Fairley, *Fun is our Business. The story of Barry's Amusements* (Newtownards: Colourpoint Books, 2006), pp. 195-209.

Picture Credits

Pages 6-7 Map of Cave Hill Country Park. Based on a drawing kindly provided by Belfast Parks.

Page 9 Postcard of Carr's Glen mill.

Page 10 Postcard of Carr's Glen.

Page 11 Carr's Glen mill buildings. Reproduced with permission from *The Irish News and Belfast Morning News* 19 March 1954.

Page 13 Photograph of the Moore family and friends provided by Sam Moore.

Page 14 Walkers on the track of the old wagonway above Ballysillan Road. Picture provided by Cathleen Arthurs.

Page 16 Photographs given to Pat Jenkins by Peggy Blair.

Page 17 Photographs given to Pat Jenkins by Peggy Blair and photograph of the terrace of cottages provided by Sam Moore.

Page 19 Daddystown photograph provided by Sam Moore.

Page 21 Photograph of Scouts on the Lines just above the Ballysillan Road provided by Fred Rankin.

Page 23 Moore family picture provided by Sam Moore.

Page 24 Tommy Beattie picture by Jim Jenkins.

Page 26 Friends at Daddystown by Jim Jenkins.

Page 27 Photograph of the Lines provided by Fred Rankin.

Page 28 Ballysillan Bridge picture provided by Jim Jenkins.

Page 29 Picture of Belfast Castle from the Lawrence Collection. Reproduced courtesy of the National Library of Ireland.

Page 33 Photograph provided by Jean Martin.

Page 36 View from Cave Hill provided by Harry Porter.

Page 38 View of the tower at Belfast Castle by the author.

Page 40 Stone staircase at Belfast Castle by the author.

Page 43 Chapel and Belfast Castle from the Lawrence Collection. Reproduced courtesy of the National Library of Ireland.

Page 44 Interior of the chapel of the Resurrection. Bigger Collection photographs number 39, Central Library, Belfast. Reproduced by kind permission of Libraries NI.

Page 46 Photograph of Mr Armstrong provided by Heather Marion Swan.

Page 47 Gamekeeper's cottage picture provided by Harry Porter.

Page 48 Drawing of the gate lodge by J. J. Phillips. Reproduced with permission of the Trustees of National Museums Northern Ireland.

Page 49 Gargoyle on gate lodge. Photograph by the author.

Page 52 Post office and gate lodge. Photograph provided by Heather Marion Swan.

Page 54 Martlett Towers. Picture from Belfast Parks archives.

Page 57 Map created by Maura Pringle for the Forest of Belfast.

Page 58 Martlett Row. Picture provided by Winnie Arbuthnot.

Page 61 Hill House. Picture from Belfast Parks archives.

Page 63 Grand staircase, Bellevue. Picture provided by John Fisher, Belfast Zoo.

Page 64 Postcard.

Page 68 Cages at the old zoo. Picture provided by John Fisher, Belfast Zoo.

Page 69 The old zoo entrance in 1978. Picture provided by John Fisher, Belfast Zoo.

Contributors

Winnie Arbuthnot. It is 80 years, the third of February 1930 since I came here, into this house on the Antrim Road. We moved from Glengormley on the Antrim line, I don't know why my parents moved here, they didn't really talk much about it. My father was a motor mechanic by trade. I was three when we moved here.

Cathleen Arthurs. I was born in Ben Vista Terrace, that's directly opposite Waterworks, in 1918 and lived on the Antrim Road until recent years, now I am in south Belfast. I am a member of the Belfast Field Naturalists' Club, though only for the last 20 years. I always liked the out-of-doors, with the Club I was places all over Ireland that I never thought I would ever see. Now I can't walk far, but I go to the lectures.

Irene Bell. We were at Cliftonville and went to live up on the Antrim Road, number 759, on the 8 May 1935. This house was built in 1932. I was 14, coming up to 15 at that time. When I was at school we spent a lot of time climbing Cave Hill. Easter holidays, every day, up to the top of the hill and down again. A crowd of us.

Diane Hunter. I grew up in Waterloo Gardens off the Antrim Road. My first sight in the morning when I opened the curtains was Cave Hill. I do miss it a lot. My parents were very keen on walking and I had no brothers or sisters so I often used to go out with them up Cave Hill. We used to roll eggs on the hill at Easter. My husband's family lived for a while on Donegall Park Avenue so he spent a lot of time up there as a child. I was first on Cave Hill when I was four or five, in the late 1930s. I was one of the founder members of the Cave Hill Conservation Campaign and at one stage meetings were held in my house.

Pat and Jim Jenkins. Pat – I was born 1928 in Australia, but moved to Belfast when 6 years old when the Depression was at its height and moved into granny and granddad's house on the Crumlin Road, a huge eight bedroom house almost directly opposite the Mater Hospital. Jim – I was born in 1923 and except for 14 years have always lived in the Cavehill Road area. We were married in 1949 and have both been involved in the North Belfast Historical Society. Now we live in Sunningdale Gardens and have a view of Cave Hill from the back window.

Alan Jones. I started to work for Belfast Parks in 1972. I started in Ormeau Park on a five-year apprenticeship and then took on the job of propagator, responsible for growing all the bedding plants for parks. I had that job for four or five years. In the early 1980s I became foreman at Belfast Castle and I have since worked as a manager at a number of parks in Belfast and now, in 2010, I am taking early retirement.

Jean Martin. I grew up at Broomhill Park and went to school at Richmond Lodge. My only memory of being on Cave Hill when I was a child was when I was at school and a very nice teacher who taught us French, she lived up on the Antrim Road and she took the whole class for a walk up Cave Hill and then down again for tea at her mother's house. That was the only time I was on Cave Hill apart from when I was a Wren at the castle during the war.

Bertie McClure. I was born in Meyrick Park right beside Carr's Glen and went up the glen from when I was a small boy, we used to bring home pussy willows and blackberries, it was our playground and perfectly safe. I was born in 1938 so this would have been in the war years. I first started to go regularly to Daddystown when I was around 13 or 14. I didn't go back for years, I wanted to remember the area as it was, as a good memory, though I have taken my children there.

Roy McConnell. At the age of eight I wanted to get into the Boys' Brigade but I was too young and I joined the Cubs. The Scout leader's brother, Jim Orchin, lived near me in the Shankill and I started going up the hill, we had an outdoor headquarters on Cave Hill at Daddystown. My father had also been in the 29th Scouts.

Sam Moore. I was brought up in the Belfast area, we moved about a bit. My grandparents were living in Oldpark and somehow through the Mission Hall my grandmother found out that a cottage at Daddystown was available. We went up there all the time.

Harry Porter. For the first 28 years of my life I lived within 250 yards of the Boys' Model School. As a young boy Carr's Glen, Cave Hill and the Belfast Castle Estate were my playground. For the past 38 years I have been only a 10-minute drive away from Bellevue and I am a regular visitor to the area. I have been a member of the 76th North Belfast Scout Group (Joanmount Methodist) for over 50 years and still take my Cub Scout pack to the Cave Hill Country Park for outdoor activities.

Margaret Redpath. I was born near Holy Cross Chapel on the Crumlin Road and apart from a brief spell in the country have lived in north Belfast all my life. I was one of the founder members of Cave Hill Campaign and I helped on the Belfast Hills walks in the early 1990s – I manned one of the staging posts and gave out soup and rolls.

Heather Marion Swan. I was born in July 1938 in the Cave Hill Post Office and went to B.R.A. Prep. next door. I left school at 16 and went into Jacob's Biscuits in the Accounts Department and later joined the Belfast Savings Bank, Carlisle Circus. I had to leave when I married Tony. My husband, as a boy, saw the Cave Hill from his bedroom window, not realizing that one day he would marry a girl from the Cave Hill and that we would live most of our married life in its shadow. We have two children, Zoë Amanda and Julian Francis Ralph.

John Swindell. I am from the Shankill and I used to come to the zoo as a kid and with my brothers walk over Cave Hill, from Ballysillan right over. I got a job looking after the grounds at Bellevue in the old zoo and then I became a keeper at the zoo.

Brendan Toland. I had been at Belfast Castle in the 70s, at a social event – I was at the College of Business Studies they used to run social events there – and I was at a wedding at the castle in the early 1980s. I started work with Belfast City Council in 1994, I became the manager of both Belfast Castle and Malone House, and I have been here ever since, and have pretty much loved every moment of it.

Craig Wallace. I was born in east Belfast so the castle was not really known to me but the zoo was. When the zoo opened in 1933-34 we always went at least once a year. With my mother, my aunt and my cousin we gazed at the animals in the cages. I became interested in the castle when I was director of parks. My legs won't allow me to go up Cave Hill now, I am not a great walker now, I'm afraid.